SOLOMON SCHECHTER ACADEMY
LIBRARY
5555 COTE ST. LUC RD.

מדרשה ע״ש שניאור זלמן שכטר

**Académie
Solomon Schechter
Academy**

This book was donated to
the library in honour of
Rosa Finestone by Mrs. E.
Green.

October 1980.

HORSES

by Moira Duggan

Photography
by Walter D. Osborne

Golden Press • New York
Western Publishing Company, Inc.
Racine, Wisconsin

636.1
Dug
c. 2

Contents

**Golden, A Golden Guide®, Golden Press® and Goldencraft®
are trademarks of Western Publishing Company, Inc.**

© Copyright 1974, 1972 by Western Publishing Company, Inc. and The Ridge
Press, Inc. All rights reserved, including rights of reproduction and use in any
form or by any means, including the making of copies by any photo process,
or by any electronic or mechanical device, printed or written or oral, or re-
cording for sound or visual reproduction, or for use in any knowledge retrieval
system or device, unless permission in writing is obtained from the copyright
proprietor. Designed and produced by The Ridge Press, Inc. Printed in the U.S.A.
by Western Publishing Company, Inc. Published by Golden Press, New York, N.Y.
Library of Congress Catalog Card Number: 77–169256.

Picture Credits
American Museum of Natural
History: 9, 11
Art Reference Bureau: 4–5
Baltimore Museum of Art: 44, 45
British Museum copyright: 42–43
Connemara Pony Society: 126 bottom
Culver Pictures: 50–51, 136, 138
Robert Elman: 128–129
Freudy Photos: 92–93, 97, 104,
126 top
Library of Congress: 90
Metropolitan Museum of Art: 85
National Museum of Racing: 46
New York Historical Society,
New York City: 76
Walter D. Osborne: 7, 16–17, 21, 24,
25, 27, 28–29, 31, 32, 34, 37, 39,
40–41, 47, 48–49, 52–53, 56–57, 58,
60–61, 63, 65, 68–69, 72–73, 77, 78,
80, 81, 83, 86, 89, 91, 94–95, 99, 101,
102, 106, 108–109, 111, 112–
113, 114–115, 116, 119, 120–121, 123,
124, 130, 131, 132–133, 140–
141, 143, 144 bottom, 146, 147,
148, 151, 155
Woolaroc Museum: 144 top
Yale University Art Gallery: 66

1 | History of the Horse

Since the time the horse was domesticated by man, well before the beginning of recorded history, it has proved more useful and more important in the progress of civilization than any other animal. Horses pulled plows, carried armies to war, moved goods to market, and right up to the present century were man's primary means of transportation. The horse breeds of today descend from those cart horses and cavalry mounts of ancient civilizations and indeed from the earliest domesticated animals of the genus *Equus*.

Each breed has its distinctive conformation, due partly to random natural factors, and partly to the practice of selective breeding, whereby a horse type acquires the characteristics it needs for peak performance in its particular job. Chapters in this guide trace the origin and development of the most popular modern breeds.

Predictions that the horse would become extinct as a result of mechanization have proved mistaken. No longer a "beast of burden," the horse is increasing in popularity as a source of enjoyment to people in many ways. Race horses are the athletes of the equine world; the Thoroughbreds of flat-track racing and the Standardbreds of harness racing draw millions of people yearly to tracks throughout the United States. Horse shows, for which many people school and ride their own horses, are a growing pastime both for participants and spectators. The stock horse, still in use for working cattle in the West, also is a star performer at Western shows and rodeos. And there is the family pleasure horse, which can be stabled in simple backyard quarters. A recent horse census showed a surprising increase in the number of families maintaining a horse for fun and exercise.

WHY THE HORSE IS SPECIAL

The horse is useful to man because of its tendency to move forward when urged to do so—its "excitability to motion." Equally important, the horse can be educated to respond in highly controlled ways to the urgings of its rider or driver. As directed, it will move fast or slow, turn this way or that, step in different gaits, jump over obstacles, etc. The primary means of controlling a horse is a bit which is placed crosswise in the horse's mouth and to which reins are attached. A rider or driver manipulates the reins so as to exert pressures on the bit and the horse responds to these pressures as it has been trained to do. A rider also uses his body to control the horse, through leg pressures and shifts of weight. The modern horse, then, is foremost an animal to be ridden (or driven). This aptitude, simply expressed in Latin, provided its scientific name, *Equus caballus.*

Preceding pages: Fragment
of Parthenon frieze shows Greek cavalry
riding bareback. Above: At rider's
command, Lippizan stallion performs levade.

EVOLUTION OF THE HORSE

Paleontologists believe that the horse evolved on the North American continent. For the sake of simplification, it is possible to pick out five key stages in the evolutionary process, each one showing increased height and greater development of mouth and hoofs.

First stage is the "dawn horse," *Eohippus* of the Hyracotherium family of leaf-browsing mammals. *Eohippus* was a shy little animal about 11 inches high. Its hind feet had only three working toes, the middle one somewhat enlarged so that the defenseless creature could take flight quickly. It lived in the Paleocene period, more than 65 million years ago.

In the Oligocene period, approximately 40 million years ago, appeared *Mesohippus*, a deer-like animal whose feet had large middle toes. It had a strongly developed jaw and, like *Eohippus*, it was a leaf-browser.

During the Miocene epoch, which ended ten million years ago, the ancestors of the horse changed their method of feeding from browsing leaves to grazing grass. This was necessitated as the face of the land changed gradually from forest to plains. The open plains environment also developed fleetness in those animals whose survival depended more on flight than on concealment. *Merychippus*, an animal about the size of a Shetland pony, illustrates the adaptations that came about during the Miocene period. Its neck was longer to allow grazing, and it was equipped with teeth capable of chewing the coarse plains grass. The side digits of its three-toed feet were too small to touch the ground.

The next eight million years, the Pliocene period, produced a true horse-type, the donkey-sized *Pliohippus*, whose feet

8

Two leaf-browsing ancestors
of modern horse: Speedy, foot-high
Eohippus (above) and
deer-like *Mesohippus* (right).

had a single large toe, or hoof; the useless side toes of its close ancestors had disappeared.

Equus, the root from which all later horse stocks branch out, finally appeared in the Pleistocene period, present epoch of geological time, which began one million years ago. Skeletal remains found in the southwestern United States show that this wild horse was much like the animal we know today, with completely developed hoofs.

About 10,000 years ago, *Equus* vanished from North America, not to return until the Spanish explorers and their excellent horses landed in the 16th century. Why the horse disappeared is not fully known; probably it was due to a combination of adverse factors including the ice age, over-kill by prehistoric hunters, and famine. Survivors emigrated to Asia over the land bridge that once existed at what is now the Bering Strait. Migration of horse ancestors had occurred in several of the earlier geological epochs, before *Equus* itself covered the route in the Pleistocene period. These early animals became extinct; only *Equus* persisted in Asia and Europe, adapting to highly diverse environments.

The horses that evolved in colder climates tended to be heavy and coarse; such was *Equus robustus,* a lumbering horse native to the forests of Europe. Descendants of these cold-climate horses are today called cold-blooded horses and include such different animals as the great draft breeds and Shetland and Icelandic ponies. In contrast, hot and arid areas produced small light horses such as *Equus agilis,* the horse of the North African plains. These species became the ancestors of today's so-called hot-blooded breeds, which include the Arabian and the Barb (Moroccan) horse.

Evolving single toe (or hoof)   11
showed on *Merychippus* (top) whose side
toes had no function, and on later
Pliohippus, which had no side toes at all.

DOMESTICATION AND EARLY USES

When man learned to hunt and kill animals for food he developed a definite taste for horseflesh; at a single prehistoric campsite in France the skeletal remains of some 100,000 horses have been excavated. It was only when man became a stationary dweller and a herder of animals that he learned the value of the horse as a beast of burden. The horse's combination of strength, agility, and learning power made it far too useful to be slaughtered for food and far more versatile than animals that had earlier been domesticated, such as the ass and the ox. The earliest archaeological evidence of the horse as a domesticated animal dates to about 4000 B.C. This was in Sialk, a community on the western edge of the Persian desert.

There has been some question as to whether man drove the horse before he learned to ride it. The argument that early horses were too small to be ridden seems false; excavated skeletons indicate that early horses were the equal in size of today's Arabian, which though not large is capable of carrying a heavy rider without tiring.

It is certain however that the horse in harness had a far greater impact on the progress of civilization than the horse with rider. Agriculture, commerce, and conquest all depended on horse-drawn vehicles. And of these, it was the war chariot —more than the merchant's cart—that helped spread early civilizations.

Ancient warfare depended on mobility, and this the horse provided. Horses were used with special effectiveness by the Hittites, an aggressive Persian people whose conquests made them the ruling power in Western Asia around 1400

12

Awesome speed and mobility
was advantage of Hittites'
light three-man war chariots, shown
here in Egyptian relief carving.

B.C. Historians of the horse have credited the early Hittites with developing the Arabian breed. Certainly they were very sophisticated horsemen, yet it seems that they may have learned much about the arts of horsemanship from the Mitanni, a group situated to the southeast of them. Detailed instructions for the care and training of horses were handed down on tablets by a Mitanni named Kikkuli, in service to Hittite rulers. These instructions are astonishing in their knowledge and exactness—about the distance and speed of daily exercise, the manner of cooling out and rubdown, the kind and amount of fodder, etc. Such expertise could have come only from centuries of work with horses, and this may have to be credited to some earlier culture than that of the Hittites, possibly that of the Mittani.

Hittite charioteers made excellent use of the flat, open terrain of the North African and Near Eastern deserts. Their

assaults were made at overpowering speed by three-man chariots rolling on light, six-spoke wheels.

The Greeks fought their wars in landscape too varied and mountainous for effective use of chariots, so they developed the horse as a cavalry mount. Miltiades, Philip of Macedon, and Alexander the Great won amazing victories largely through their skillful and imaginative use of cavalry.

The Romans also conquered on horseback after learning from their brilliant Carthaginian enemy, Hannibal, the value of a superbly trained cavalry mounted on fast and durable desert horses.

14

"Great horse" of medieval warfare was bred to huge size and heavily caparisoned for use in tournaments and combat.

Warfare in the Middle Ages was carried on by nobles riding heavy horses. Never has the art of combat been more idealized, nor the war horse more glorified. After modern weaponry made the Great Horse obsolete, it was retired to peaceful service on the roads and farms of Europe and Britain.

A WHO'S WHO OF HORSES

Certain horses have shared the heroic stature of their masters. Alexander the Great was so devoted to his fiery mount Bucephalus that he built a city in the horse's name and buried him in an alabaster tomb.

El Morazillo, ridden by Hernando Cortez in leading the conquest of Mexico, was deified and worshipped by the Mexican Indians for two centuries after his death.

A celebrated war horse of more recent times was the splendid gray ridden by Robert E. Lee in commanding the Confederate Army. Traveler is buried on the campus of Washington & Lee University in Virginia.

The horses of mythology, though fictional, deserve mention with the famous equines of the epic past. To the Greeks, horses symbolized the blessings of the gods, and the Greek myths include tales of two marvelous steeds: Arion, horse of Hercules, and Pegasus, the winged horse of Bellerophon.

In the ancient sagas of many lands, the horse is often courier between heaven and earth, or bearer of heroes to the hereafter. Norse heroes were borne to Valhalla by the horses of the Valkyries. And Mohamet is said to have ascended on El Barat, "a fine-limbed, high-standing horse, strong in frame and with a coat glossy as marble," a description of the ideal horse as true for today as it was in ancient times.

15

2 | First Facts About Horses

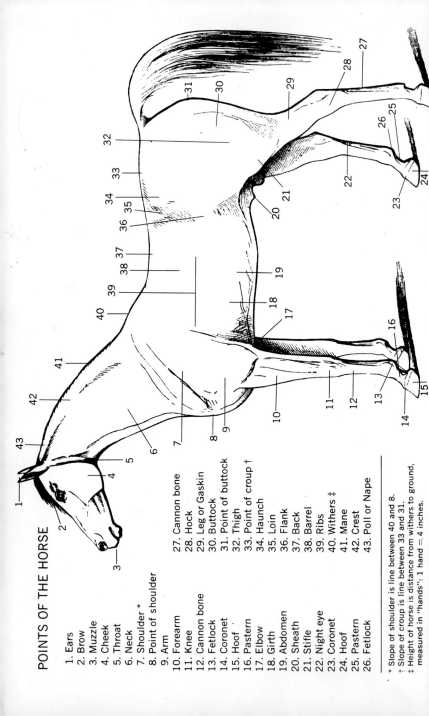

POINTS OF THE HORSE

1. Ears
2. Brow
3. Muzzle
4. Cheek
5. Throat
6. Neck
7. Shoulder *
8. Point of shoulder
9. Arm
10. Forearm
11. Knee
12. Cannon bone
13. Fetlock
14. Coronet
15. Hoof
16. Pastern
17. Elbow
18. Girth
19. Abdomen
20. Sheath
21. Stifle
22. Night eye
23. Coronet
24. Hoof
25. Pastern
26. Fetlock
27. Cannon bone
28. Hock
29. Leg or Gaskin
30. Buttock
31. Point of buttock
32. Thigh
33. Point of croup †
34. Haunch
35. Loin
36. Flank
37. Back
38. Barrel
39. Ribs
40. Withers ‡
41. Mane
42. Crest
43. Poll or Nape

* Slope of shoulder is line between 40 and 8.
† Slope of croup is line between 33 and 31.
‡ Height of horse is distance from withers to ground, measured in "hands": 1 hand = 4 inches.

CONFORMATION

A sound and attractive horse of any breed is pleasing to the eye and shows quality in the "points of conformation." Below are some of the ideals that most light-horse breeds have in common.

Croup: sloping or nearly horizontal, according to function of breed, but generally long and muscular.

Legs: positioned for a square, solid stance. Forelegs, seen from the front, are straight, with feet set about a hoof's breadth apart. Hind legs, viewed from behind, are straight and perpendicular to the body. Bones are flat, not rounded. Tendons large and well defined. No puffiness in joints.

Pasterns: neither too long nor too short; angle of about 60 degrees is ideal for shock-absorbing function.

Hoofs: rounded, with no cracks or rings.

Hindquarters: clean-cut and muscular.

Back: well blended with front and hindquarters and in good proportion; short is ideal of most breeds.

Chest: broad and deep for good lung capacity.

Shoulders: sloping (i.e., line from withers to point of shoulder), not straight or steep. Good angulation of shoulder and arm provides springiness and resistance to shocks.

Neck: long in most fine breeds, well set into shoulders.

Eyes: prominent, wide-set, expressive of good disposition.

Head: proportioned for balance, i.e., large on a short neck, small on a long neck. Bone structure well defined. Forehead broad and flat, and profile straight or slightly dished. (A Roman nose is characteristic of draft breeds.)

Ears: set wide and forward on forehead, alertly carried.

Hair: an indicator of health; it should be fine, vigorous, with natural sheen, and full in the tail.

Pages 16 and 17: Wild
horses on Nevada plain at dawn.
Tough and scrubby animals
are descended from domesticated horses.

COLORS*

The solid colors are classed as follows.

Black (blk): a rare color, not to be confused with very dark bay or brown; there are no light areas.

Brown (br): brown horses may be anything from deep brown to near-black, with light areas at muzzle and eyes.

Bay (b): a range of reddish hues from *sandy bay* (light shades), to *blood bay* (red shades), to *mahogany bay* (dark shades); distinguishing characteristic of bay horses is that mane and tail, and often lower legs, are black, and ear tips are edged with black.

Chestnut (ch): a range of reddish brown hues, with mane and tail of same color or lighter.

Gray (gr): a blending of white and black hairs; depending on proportion of dark to light, horse may be a very dark gray or almost white. At birth these animals are dark; they lighten gradually as they mature.

White: true white is rare: such a horse is usually an albino.

Palomino (p): a range of golden colors, from cream to orange; mane and tail should be lighter than the body, from silver to flaxen. White leg markings are common.

Roan (rn): a fairly uniform mixture of hairs of different colors: *strawberry roan* (chestnut with white hairs); *blue roan* (black, white and red hairs); *red roan* (bay with white).

Dun (d): a range of dull tans including grayish *mouse dun,* yellowish *buckskin dun,* and a creamy color called *Isabella;* all have a black mane and tail.

Spotted or particolored horses are of two types:

Piebald (p.b.)—black and white

Skewbald (skbld)—white and any color except black

*abbreviations are standard usage for show catalogs, etc.

Blaze: a large patch of white on forehead.

Star: a small white patch on forehead.

Strip: a patch extending from forehead part-way down the face.

Stripe: a thin line of white extending from forehead to the nose or lip. A "calf-faced" horse is one with a predominantly white face.

Snip: a white or skin-colored spot on the lip or nose.

LEG MARKINGS

Stocking: white marking on leg, as high as knee of the foreleg, or hock of hind leg.

Half-stocking: white on leg about midway to knee or hock.

Sock: white marking from hoof to fetlock.

Spotted hide (skewbald) is
breed requirement of Appaloosa (above)
Pintos and Palominos are other
types distinguished by coloration.

DEVELOPING THE BREEDS

"Breeds" within the horse family mean those strains that have been cultivated by man and which reproduce true to type from generation to generation. Horses such as the Mongolian ass and the zebra are not breeds but wild species. Almost all the so-called "wild horses" now existing, such as the American mustang and the many uncultivated pony races, are descendants of once domesticated animals that returned to the wild at some time in the past.

Breeding—the gradual improvement of an animal type through selective mating—has been practiced by horsemen for many centuries and is now a highly sophisticated science. The breeder seeks to produce foals that are sound, vigorous, and good specimens of the breed's characteristics. He selects animals to be mated on the basis of their good health, the quality of the offspring they have already produced, and any special characteristics he may hope to see passed on to the foal—for example, speed, jumping ability, or a docile temperament. He avoids breeding a stallion and a mare that have the same fault of conformation, soundness, or disposition. The breeder also takes into account the horses' bloodlines—their ancestries—which are given in the stud book or registry of the breed. He notes particularly the qualities of the parents, grandparents, and great-grandparents on each side and the quality of their descendants.

This process of selective breeding has developed many of the modern breeds described in this guide, including the Standardbred, the American Saddle Horse, the Thorough-bred, and the Quarter Horse, and is quickly improving horses such as the Appaloosa and the Paint.

22

BREED TERMS

Blood horse: term sometimes used for a horse of the Thoroughbred breed.

Cross: a mating between horses of two different breeds, or of different family lines within a breed.

Dam: a mare, the mother of a foal.

Family: within a breed, a strain with its own particular characteristics and line of descent (as the Denmarks, Chiefs, and Highlanders of the American Saddle Horse breed).

Foal: a newborn horse; a mare "foals" when she gives birth.

Foundation Sire (or Mare): a stallion, or mare, whose progeny have been a major contribution in the formation of a breed.

Gelding: a castrated male horse.

Get: a foal, the offspring of a mating; also, all the offspring of a particular stallion.

Line breeding: mating together the descendants of one superior animal so that the common ancestor's desirable characteristics will be standardized over successive generations of progeny; the practice by which breed or family characteristics are fixed. Mating of near-related relatives, such as brother and sister, or sire and daughter, is called *inbreeding*.

Prepotency: quality of a sire whose characteristics appear consistently and to a marked degree in his offspring.

Purebred: a horse of a recognized breed whose male and female ancestors over many generations have all been registered animals.

Sire: a stallion, the father of a foal.

Stud: a stallion used for breeding; also, a breeding farm.

Stud book: the record book of a breed, naming sire and dam of each horse registered.

LIFE HISTORY

A horse is born after a gestation period of 11 months. Within a half hour or so after birth, the long-legged baby learns to stand up and to feed on its mother's milk, its chief nourishment for about the first six months of life. After this, as a "weanling," it has its milk teeth and feeds on grains and grass. Growth continues to age five and full weight is reached at seven. From weaning through age four, the young female is called a *filly,* the male a *colt;* after that they become *mare* and *horse* (or *stallion*) respectively.

Properly handled and cared for, a horse should be fully serviceable for perhaps ten or more years after reaching maturity. Since it ages at the rate of three years for every one in the human life span, at 21 it is the equal in age of a 63-year-old man. A horse that lives past 30—as some do—is in extreme old age.

Horse farm scenes: Morgan brood mares, resting foal, and young Standardbred gamboling in Bluegrass pasture.

INTELLIGENCE

The question of intelligence applies no less to the horse than to any other animal. How much, if anything, it "knows" remains a matter for scientific investigation. It is certain, however, that the sensory system of the horse supplies it with much information. Its sight is extremely keen, with such a wide angle of vision that it can see almost straight behind. Extraordinary, too, are its hearing and smell, its reflexes and motor co-ordination. In addition, the horse has remarkable memory powers. Like the famous Lippizan stallions of the Spanish Riding School of Vienna, it can be trained to perform involved routines. Like the cutting horse of the Western range, it can learn to anticipate and out-maneuver the dodgings of a runaway steer. Its excellent memory can be a liability, too, for any reminder of a bad scare can cause a horse to react violently.

By nature, the horse is timid. A vicious horse is either a quirk of nature or the product of mishandling. The stallion's tendency to aggressive, even hostile, behavior proceeds from his nature and function as a sire, and is not a cause of concern to experienced horsemen. Some types of horses, it is true, are less good-natured than others and require a firmer hand in training and handling.

Thus, the personality of any individual horse is an amalgam of several influences: his breed characteristics, the treatment he receives, and his individual make-up. A horse may be high-strung or nonchalant, "giving" or laggard, quick or slow to learn. He has enough intelligence to be useful to man in many different ways, but not enough to realize that he has the advantage in physical strength.

26

Cowboy lets savvy
Appaloosa cutting horse turn
reluctant steer in
direction of corral gate.

GAITS

The way a horse steps or runs is called a gait. The basic natural gaits are the walk, trot, and gallop; in addition, there are many variations on these which horses can be trained to perform. An aptitude for a certain gait has been responsible for the development of many breeds. The Tennessee Walking Horse is a prime example of a horse bred for its gait; riding a sure-footed and restful Walker, a man inspecting a plantation can spend an entire day in the saddle without becoming tired and without damaging crops as he moves among the plant rows. Another example is the Thoroughbred race horse, developed for galloping swiftly over comparatively short distances.

28

Show horse drawing
fine-harness rig exhibits
crisply elevated
action in trotting gait.

A gait may be generally termed "high" or "low." The Thoroughbred has a "low" action—there is only as much elevation of the feet as is needed for his great pendular strides. The English Hackney and the American Saddle Horse have extremely "high" actions that are intended mainly for show. These breeds are exaggerated examples, however. With any horse, training is required to develop poised and good-looking action, even in the walk. More extensive training goes into developing highly styled, modified gaits, such as the canter in place, the pace, and the rack. For certain gaits, such as the slow canter, the rider "collects" his horse, controlling its impulse to move freely. When collected, the horse appears poised, eager, co-ordinated, and compact.

The WALK is an even gait of four beats, with the feet striking the gound in sequence. There is little elevation of the feet. The American Saddle Horse and the Tennessee Walking Horse exhibit the *running walk,* which is a walking gait, but much faster and with a much more extended stride.

The TROT is a two-beat gait in which diagonal front and rear feet strike the ground at the same time. It can be performed at varying speeds: as a slow and easy gait, as the snappy, quick trot used in showing, and as the reaching, flat-out stride of the racing trotter.

The GALLOP is a springing, three-beat gait in which the feet hit the ground in the following order (on a left lead): left foreleg, right hind leg, and simultaneously the left hind and right forelegs. In the racer's extended gallop, there is a moment when all four of the horse's feet are off the ground. One such sequence can cover up to 24 feet.

The CANTER follows the same sequence as the gallop but the cadence is slower and the hind legs do not propel the horse as strongly as in the gallop. It is a rhythmic and collected gait for pleasure riding. A Western version, using the same foot placement, is the *lope,* well named for its free, swinging, low-action motion.

The PACE is an artificial gait used almost exclusively in harness racing. Legs of either side advance together: left foreleg and left hind leg in one beat; right feet in second beat.

Top: Ground-covering
gallop of Thoroughbred race horse.
Right: Collected canter
demonstrated by Lippizan stallion.

3 | The Arabian

This is the horse of the Arabian desert, an ancient breed famed for its loyalty, intelligence, and endurance. In the colorful lore of Arabian horses, one tale sums up their qualities. It concerns the origin of the five major strains within the breed and tells of Salaman, a famous Arab horseman of the 17th century B.C., whose herd had traveled the desert many days without water. When water at last was reached and the horses were crowding toward it to drink, Salaman was forced to summon them back with the call to battle. Five mares obeyed, resisting the urge to slake their thirst. These noble animals—called *Al Khamseh* ("the five") —became the chief foundation mares of the Arabian horse family. Or so the legend goes.

Owners of Arabian horses prize their beauty and spirit under saddle. This is the greatest of the world's pure breeds, and it has added quality to every breed with which it has been crossed.

Arabian yearling should
possess spirit and stamina,
traditional qualities
of world's oldest breed.

THE ARABIAN LOOK

Size runs 14 to 15 hands, though the horses will grow larger in favorable environments.

Coat is silky, with exceptional sheen. Usual colors are brown, bay, chestnut, and gray.

Legs are clean, with slender bones and prominent tendons.

Pasterns are springy, slightly longer than Thoroughbred's.

Croup is broad, flat.

Barrel is short and compact, with well-sprung ribs.

Withers are not very pronounced.

Neck is flexible, muscular, and well arched into the head.

Head is delicate, often wedge-shaped, tapering to a fine muzzle; forehead is prominent and profile often concave or ''dished.''

Ears are small and curved, with inward-pointing tips.

Eyes are large, round, set low and wide apart, with protruding appearance.

Jaw is strong, with well-defined, disc-like cheekbones.

HISTORY

Did the Arabian originate as a wild native horse or was it brought to the desert from the East? Importation—perhaps by the Hittites—seems the likeliest explanation. Yet archaeology has shown that the lower region of Arabia, the Nedj, was once green and well watered, and its underlying rock is limestone, a factor in the development of sound bones. In such conditions a native horse could have flourished.

One phase of Arabian lore seems certain: the existence of *Al Khamseh,* the foundation mares of the five families from which subfamilies later branched out. In this breed mares have greater importance than stallions. Lineage, unlike that of other breeds, is traced through the dam side. Purebred Arabian mares were so carefully guarded that until recent times it was almost impossible to bring one out of Arabia. (Empress Catherine the Great of Russia was able to acquire a number of matched stallions and mares.)

A mare was a Bedouin's most treasured possession. He rode her confidently into battle, sheltered her in his tent at night (since her keen hearing gave early warning of approaching danger), and sometimes used her milk for nourishment.

The prime consideration of Arabian breeders has always been to keep the bloodlines pure. This purity and the absence of undesirable characteristics may account for the exceptional ability of Arabians to transmit desirable qualities when crossed with other breeds. Fortunately, modern breeders throughout the world have maintained the purity of the Arabian. The American registry, for example, permits no outcrossing with other breeds and scrutinizes all entries, even conducting blood tests if lineage is in doubt.

Aahdin, Grand
Champion Reserve Arabian stallion,
well illustrates
characteristics of his breed.

ARABIAN CHARACTERISTICS

Many of the unique qualities of this breed are based on structural advantages. Bedouins claim, for example, that the Arabian's intelligence is accounted for by its large brain pan. That is why a wide forehead, or *jibbah*, is especially valued.

The Arab's compactness comes from having fewer vertebrae than other horses. The ordinary horse has 6 lumbar (ribless) vertebrae, 19 ribbed vertebrae, and 18 tail vertebrae. The Arabian, in contrast, has 5 lumbar vertebrae, 18—in some cases 17—pairs of ribs, and 16 tail vertebrae.

The legs of the Arabian are very strong and resistant to disease and injury. The bones, though slender, are ivory-hard, and the tendons have steely resilience.

The smooth gaits typical of the Arab are attributed to the well-inclined, shock-absorbing slope of the shoulders; and the nearly tireless propelling power of the hindquarters is due partly to their unusual length in relation to the short back that is characteristic of the breed.

Another asset, contributing to stamina and freedom from respiratory ailments, is the very large windpipe of the Arabian, with a wide entrance at the throat.

An unusually wide angle of vision is afforded to the Arabian by the wide spacing and prominence of its eyes. The Arabian's teeth are also unique, much smaller and finer than in horses of other types.

The Arab's dark skin is an adaptation developed over generations of exposure to desert sun, and its small size, too, is the result of evolving in an environment where forage is sparse.

36

Versatile Arabian
is often shown, like these,
in Western-class
events of horse shows.

37

THE ARABIAN IN AMERICA

The mark of Arabian blood is clear in many modern breeds including the Morgan, Hackney, and Quarter Horse. It was the key contribution in the formation of the Thoroughbred, whose foundation sires—Matchem, Eclipse, and Herod—were of Eastern ancestry. In England, breeding of Thoroughbred sires to mares of strong Arab blood was continued for generations with excellent results: Thoroughbred descendants of the Darley Arabian won 87 percent of the runnings of the English Derby over a period of 127 years.

The Darley Arabian also contributed to the evolution of America's Standardbred trotters and pacers. A Darley descendant, Imported Messenger, was great-grandfather of Hambletonian 10, a chief Standardbred foundation sire.

Arabians came to America in various ways. In the late 1800's several were imported by a breeder named Randolph Huntington who hoped to create a "national" horse of a refined and distinctive type, using the great trotter Henry Clay as foundation sire.

Forty-five desert horses were sent by the Turkish government to the Chicago World's Fair of 1893 as part of an elaborate show. Fire and other disasters befell the troupe in Chicago and the horses that survived were sold. Eight were of the purest Arabian strains, and two of these became foundation horses in the American Registry.

Total number of Arabians registered is more than 70,000; (76 were registered in 1908 when the Arabian Horse Club of America was formed). Though generally regarded as pleasure horses, some Arabians are being bred for stock work, which they do with characteristic intelligence.

Arabian's desert origins provide theme for regalia in costume-class event of show.

4 | The Thoroughbred

The Thoroughbred horse was developed in England in the 18th century as the ideal animal for racing and cross-country hunting—a horse that combined speed, stamina, and jumping ability.

Hunting and racing on horseback has been carried on in Britain as long ago as the Roman occupation, with the members of the nobility as the most enthusiastic participants. These horse sports, however, could not progress beyond the talents of the horses themselves, and it became a traditional

Preceding pages: Foal frisking with dam on Thoroughbred breeding farm. Above: 1684 horse race observed by Charles II of England.

interest of English monarchs to improve the quality of their
stock. James I promoted the breeding and training of
Eastern-blooded race horses. Charles II, "Father of the
English Turf," revitalized the Royal Stud, set up the famous
race course at New Market, even rode in races himself. In
Charles's 25-year reign (1660–85), horse racing as it is known
today began to take form. The one important element still
to come was the horse that today dominates the sport—the
Thoroughbred.

THE EASTERN PROGENITORS

Three horses, all of Eastern blood, stand at the very beginning of the Thoroughbred breed. First is the "Byerly Turk," imported to England before 1700 by a British officer, Captain Byerly. Then, around 1705, a Mr. Thomas Darley imported a stallion from Syria: the "Darley Arabian" is the second of the Thoroughbred progenitors. About 20 years later the third appeared, the "Godolphin Barb," named after his owner, the Earl of Godolphin. (The designations "Turk," "Arabian," and "Barb" refer to breeds native to Turkey, Arabia, and the Barbary Coast.)

The importance of the three horses, as time proved, was in their prepotency, their ability to pass on their own desirable qualities of speed, endurance, and refinement to generations of descendants.

44

Above left: Darley
Arabian, important Thoroughbred
ancestor. Above right:
George Stubbs portrait of Eclipse.

FOUNDATION SIRES

Horsemen developed the Thoroughbred family along blood-lines tracing back to three descendants of the Turk, the Arabian, and the Barb. The horses were Matchem, a grandson of the Godolphin Barb; Herod, a great-great-grandson of the Byerly Turk; and Eclipse, a great-great-grandson of the Darley Arabian. The three were foaled between 1748 and 1764. They established themselves as the "foundation sires" of the Thoroughbred family by their supremacy as race horses, and by the quality of their offspring. The "taproot mares" of the Thoroughbred breed were English mares of strong Eastern blood. Late in the 18th century the British General Stud Book was closed to all horses whose bloodlines did not go back through the male line either to Matchem, Herod, or Eclipse.

45

THE THOROUGHBRED LOOK

Size may reach 17 hands, and physique is lithe and clean.

Coat should be lustrous with fine-haired mane and tail.

Legs are long, especially the "drive shaft," the distance between the point of the hip and the hock on the rear legs.

Pasterns are springy to absorb shocks of galloping gait.

Croup has pronounced rise, and rump is sloping.

Withers are very pronounced.

Barrel has ribs sprung from the spine at a more downward angle than is usual with other breeds.

Chest is deep and broad to accommodate well-developed heart and lungs.

Shoulders are sloping.

Neck is long and gracefully proportioned.

Head is refined with profile straight or dished.

Bearing is spirited and delicate.

INFLUENCE ON SPORTS

The exciting talents of the Thoroughbred quickened the sporting scene in 18th-century England. Racing drew the public in ever greater numbers. (Perhaps the people took example from Queen Anne, an intrepid horsewoman and founder of the Ascot races.) And the Thoroughbreds themselves prospered, due to a change in custom from match races between just two horses to races with fields of several runners; in response to the demand for good horses, more were produced by breeders.

Meanwhile, riders to hounds found in the Thoroughbred a splendid mount for the new sport of fox hunting. Before great areas of land were cleared for agriculture. hunting had been mostly after stag or boar in woodland settings that made for fairly slow pursuit. But riding after fox in open country meant taking dozens of jumps at the gallop, and the Thoroughbred proved fully equal to the test.

Left: Two-year-old
Man o' War exhibits athletic
trim of Thoroughbred racer.
Above: Training a steeplechaser.

47

5 | Thoroughbred Racing

When importation of Thoroughbreds began in America, just after the Revolution, horse racing was already a popular sport. Match races between two horses were commonly staged on some suitable town street, or on a track carved from the surrounding woodland; the quarter-mile sprint was a popular event. The horses were usually general-purpose animals with superior speed.

Flat racing, "end-to-end" over an oval track, was inaugurated in America in 1665, when Richard Nicolls, first English governor of New York, established a course called Newmarket near what is now Belmont Park on Long Island. Here the formal racing traditions of the British were observed, and the horses were probably of the "Dutch" strain imported from Holland and bred in New England.

In 1730, an outstanding son of the Darley Arabian, Bulle

Rocke, was imported to Virginia. At this time, the Thorough-bred breed was in its formative period in England. It would be half a century before Thoroughbreds would arrive in America in any significant number.

Toward the end of the 18th century, some important Thoroughbred stallions made the voyage to the States. They included Messenger, root of the Standardbred harness-racing family and an ancestor of such great runners as the top money-winner Kelso; also Medley, Shark, and Diomed— all producers of many illustrious descendants. Diomed's son, Sir Archy, was the first important American-bred stallion. A match race between such great horses as these drew enormous crowds in the early days of the Republic. Forty thousand people thronged to see Sir Henry beat American Eclipse at the Union Race Course on Long Island in 1823.

Governor Nicolls inaugurates
racing in New York in 1665.
Horses were slower than today's
Thoroughbreds (preceding pages).

AFTER THE CIVIL WAR

As a sport, Thoroughbred racing had come into its own by the 1850's. The English practice of racing in single dashes had largely replaced the old custom of deciding a winner on the best of several heats of up to four miles each. Not only was the older method less exciting, it also made it easier for a race to be "thrown," since horses had to be held in greater control to last for such long distances.

The Civil War affected racing and breeding in many ways. Many fine animals were turned over to the Confederate Army. Breeding records were lost or destroyed, and many of the major horse-raising centers of the Southeast became inactive. However, Kentucky's Bluegrass establishment, around Lexington, survived the conflict and has since led the

At New York's Saratoga track,
horses are walked by grooms to cool
out after early morning exercise.

country in producing superior Thoroughbreds.

After the Civil War, the South lost its traditional leadership in the sport of racing. Religious feeling against the morality of wagering was one cause, the damaged economy of the South was another. The Northern states moved quickly to the forefront of racing activity, New York especially. There, in 1864, the Saratoga race course was opened as Thoroughbred racing's most splendid setting. In the 1860's and 70's new tracks were opened, including Pimlico in Maryland, the New Orleans Fair Grounds, and Churchill Downs, home of the Kentucky Derby. Great horses like Norfolk, Domino, Ben Brush, and the filly Ruthless, ran for rich purses. This was the "Golden Age" of Thoroughbred racing and it lasted to the end of the century.

RACING IN THE 20th CENTURY

As the 1900's arrived, with no strong regulation of racing activity, corrupt practices had become commonplace. Horses were doped, races were fixed, and the system of betting was in a state of disorder. A wave of reform legislation swept the States, with only Maryland and Kentucky remaining friendly to the sport. These states, home country of the Thoroughbreds, kept racing alive. At the Kentucky Derby at Churchill Downs in 1908 a machine was used for the first time which was to make it possible to erase many of the abuses in trackside betting. The "totalizator" calculated odds mechanically and made possible the pari-mutuel system, in which odds are established by the varying amounts of money that bettors put down on each entry. Mechanical odds-making legitimized betting in the eyes of lawmakers, and also opened an attractive source of revenue. Racing was saved, and leaders in the sport moved to make it as honest as possible. Today it is one of the most closely regulated sports.

Mechanization—from the starting gate to the photo-finish camera to computerized betting—has made racing more exciting. There are more than 100 flat-racing tracks operating in the United States and annual attendance is running close to 50 million. Top events are the three races for the Triple Crown—the Derby, Preakness, and Belmont Stakes, all for three-year-olds. But the true thrills of racing come from the great-hearted Thoroughbreds themselves, and the past decades have produced some immortal heroes, including Kelso, with winnings of almost $2 million; Exterminator, victor in 50 of 100 starts; and Man o' War, beaten but once in 21 races. Their will to win will never be forgotten.

54

BREEDING

The making of a Thoroughbred race horse begins even before he is born. His parents are chosen with care in the hopes that a crossing of their bloodlines will produce a foal with just the right mix of characteristics to win races. Only two out of three Thoroughbreds foaled in any one season actually make it to the turf. The sire is regarded as the more important contributor to the quality of the "get," but the dam is very important, too, not only because of her genetic contribution, but because she is the guardian and example of temperament to the foal in the first months of life.

Spring is the time for foaling. All Thoroughbreds have their first official birthday on the January 1st after the actual day of their birth. Thereafter the youngster is known as a *yearling colt* or *yearling filly* until it is two years old, when the *yearling* designation is dropped. At age five, the male will be called a *horse,* the female a *mare.* According to current practice, the Thoroughbred begins its racing career at least two years before its maturity at age four or five.

A Thoroughbred is named while it is a yearling. The owner offers a name for registration with the Jockey Club, the organization that maintains the breeding records of American Thoroughbreds. To be acceptable it must not be more than 16 letters long, nor conflict with the name of any other living, registered horse, nor be in poor taste. The name cannot be changed, even if owners change.

Whenever the Thoroughbred is raced, its jockey wears the "silks" of the horse's owner—a blouse and cap in a combination of pattern and colors belonging exclusively to that owner.

55

Thoroughbreds in pastures of Bluegrass country. A young horse is never far from its mother.

TRAINING

Training a horse for "the sport of kings" is a long and painstaking process. When only a few days old, the foal is fitted with a simple halter and taught the touch of the human hand. Months later, as a colt, he is bridled and put through some beginner's paces at the end of a 30-foot line called the longe (pronounced "lunge"). Jogging in circles around his trainer, he learns to move well in the various gaits and to respond to commands. When big enough to carry a man, he is saddled for the first time and taught to walk with rider. As training progresses, he learns to run and to overcome his timidity while maintaining proper track deportment. By age two, he has started rehearsals for real racing, working out at gradually more demanding paces and being schooled for the starting gate. Very soon he is ready for his "maiden" race.

The Thoroughbred breeding industry produces some 15,000 Thoroughbreds annually. Many horsemen are concerned that out of this crop the only horse capable of winning the Triple Crown since Citation in 1948 has been the superbly made Secretariat, winner in 1973. The economics of breeding have made it necessary for owners to start their horses racing as early as possible to regain the many thousands of dollars spent on purchase price (or sire's stud fee), training, keep, and registration fees. It may be that performance pressures are preventing the young Thoroughbreds from maturing properly and realizing their potential. However, with the breed in the hands of highly devoted horsemen, its continuing greatness seems assured.

Top: Trainers use longe line
and flexible bamboo pole in schooling
session with yearling. Left:
Exercise "boys" end workout runs.

6 | The Standardbred

HISTORY OF THE STANDARDBRED

The American custom of racing horses in harness goes back to colonial days—to the neighborly "brush" two men might have while driving their trotters to town, or to the races that sparked holiday celebrations and fairs. Just as harness racing today is vastly different from its origins, so are the horses themselves. The roadsters of early days were mostly utility horses that were also fast runners. But when trotting grew into a major sport, early in the 1800's, a more specialized type of animal was needed. In seeking to create such a horse, breeders looked to the progeny of an imported Thoroughbred stallion called Messenger, a descendant of the Darley Arabian. As Messenger's descendants multiplied it was noted that they possessed speed and were naturally inclined to the trotting gait. And indeed it was one of Messenger's grandsons, Rysdyck's Hambletonian, that in time earned recognition as foundation sire of the Standardbred family, the breed which has been developed over the past century especially for racing in the trot or pace. (A trotter advances diagonal legs at the same time; a pacer advances legs of right or left side at the same time.)

Hambletonian 10, as the stud book lists him, was foaled in 1849 in Chester, New York. His future greatness was guessed by only one person, his owner's hired man, William Rysdyck, who bought the colt for $125. Hambletonian matured an immensely strong if not very handsome horse, who in 24 years at stud sired 1,300 foals with at least 40 blazing runners among them. His stud fee rose to $500.

Of today's trotters and pacers, perhaps nine out of ten trace back to Mr. Rysdyck's bargain horse. Thoroughbred

62

blood is predominant in the breed, though Morgan and other strains have been introduced to provide ruggedness. Today's Standardbred is typically a horse of 15 or 16 hands, well muscled, especially in the legs. He is long in the barrel, with the croup often higher than the withers. His rear legs are placed well under him, and his pasterns are notably long. He inherits a tendency for either the trotting or pacing gait. His trainer's job is to develop this talent.

The term "standardbred" originally meant a horse of any breed that could trot the mile in harness within a certain standard time. The standard has lowered over the years and is now 2:20 for two-year-olds and 2:15 for older horses. If a horse meets this standard, he qualifies to run in officially recognized meets. "Standardbred" became the name for the pedigreed family of horses bred for racing in harness.

Preceding pages: Standardbred
in pre-race workout at Santa Anita.
Above: Harness horse remains
in use with Amish people of Pennsylvania.

HARNESS RACING

For the first few decades of the 19th century harness racing was fairly informal, a matter of owners challenging each other on some suitable stretch of road. If trotters were raced on tracks, it was usually under saddle. Trotting was spared the religious disapproval which closed the flat-racing tracks of the Northeast in 1802. Lawmakers reasoned that since a horse in a trotting race was not running as fast as it *could* run—in a faster gait—trotting races weren't really races and therefore were not immoral. Thus favored, the sport flourished and, by the 1840's, improved tracks and sulkies made racing in harness the preferred style for trotters. Harness racing gained in popularity up to the Civil War, but when it was resumed after the war its disorganization and crooked practices were a disgrace to the sporting scene. Through the 1860's strenuous reforms were undertaken and by 1870 a governing body had been set up that in time became the National Trotting Association. Harness racing finished out the century in a very healthy condition, honestly conducted and attracting an increasing number of breeders, owners, and fans.

Two inventions gave impetus to the sport in the late-century years. First, in 1885, the hopple was introduced to the pacing game. Though faster generally than trotters, pacers were less popular with bettors because of their tendency to break out of the pacing stride. (The trotter that breaks stride can be urged back into it; the pacer cannot.) The hopple was simply a harness that prevented the horse from running in any gait but the pace. Next, in 1895, came the light, "bike"-type sulky with pneumatic tires and ball-

bearing wheels. Pulling this vehicle, horses began shaving seconds from the records. In 1897 the two-minute mile, once thought impossible, was cracked by the pacer Star Pointer in a time of 1:59¼.

At the turn of the century the legendary pacer Dan Patch began a career that made him almost a national hero. He raced for nine years and 30 times ran the mile in under two minutes. At age nine he did it in 1:54¼, a pacing record that stood for 33 years.

Harness racing declined in the Twenties and Thirties, though the sport was kept alive at smaller tracks and fairgrounds. The Standardbreds were due for a stunning comeback, however, and it began on an evening in September, 1940, at Roosevelt Raceway on Long Island when night-time harness racing made its debut.

Pacer in full stride
is wearing hopple, harness
that restricts movement
in any gait but the pace.

Harness racing entered an era of fabulous popularity in the mid-Forties. Night racing attracted afternoon flat-track fans and people with daytime jobs. And the type of racing they saw was more exciting than before. False starts were eliminated by the automobile-mounted starting gate, introduced in 1946. The old custom of deciding a winner on the best of several heats was largely abandoned in favor of single-heat decisions. As attendance climbed, track managements enlarged and expanded their plants.

It is still a golden era for the Standardbreds. About 25 million people attend trotting and pacing races annually, spending nearly $2 billion at the betting windows. In the vintage year of 1969 Nevele Pride earned the title "fastest trotter in history" with a mile in 1:54⅘, and New Zealand-bred pacer Cardigan Bay retired at age 12 as the first Standardbred to earn a million dollars.

INSIDE HARNESS RACING

Harness racing—a sport as American as baseball—has a distinctly democratic flavor. The more aristocratic patrons of horse sports have traditionally favored Thoroughbred racing, "the sport of kings." Special to the harness scene is the close involvement of owners with the day-to-day careers of their horses. It costs much less to own and race a Standardbred than a Thoroughbred, and the harness horse has more years of track life to reward its owner's investment. Many owners are in the sport of harness racing with just one horse, while in Thoroughbred racing it is more usual for owners to command whole stables of promising runners. Also, it is not unusual for Standardbred owners to drive their horses on the track—in workouts and sometimes in races. The Standardbred has a calm disposition, and the dangers of driving one do not approach those of piloting a Thoroughbred.

Few sports performers have longer careers than sulky drivers. With luck, a man can start in his teens and retire in his seventies. Some drivers train the animals they race; many of the leading drivers are also owners and breeders. The dream success story of harness racing is that of Mr. Harrison Hoyt, a Connecticut businessman and amateur driver, who won the 1948 Hambletonian—most prestigious race of the harness world—driving Demon Hanover, a horse he had bought as a yearling and trained himself.

The breeding of trotters and pacers is on a much smaller scale than that of Thoroughbreds. There are two major establishments, several farms of important size, and a number of medium-size to small operations.

Hambletonian, foundation
sire of Standardbred breed, shown
with owner William Rysdyck
in 1865 Currier & Ives lithograph.

TRAINING THE STANDARDBRED

Training begins with the first touch of a man's hand, soon after the foal is dropped by its dam. A halter is placed on its head which it wears during the first months of life. Only as a yearling is it introduced to the pieces of the harness, first the bridle, then one by one the other straps and fastenings of the complicated rig. Next the young horse is taught to walk ahead of his trainer, guided by very long

Field rounds turn
in pacing race at California's
Santa Anita track.

reins. After a week or two of learning to turn right or left in response to the reins, he is hitched to a cart and jogged, gently and slowly in early sessions, faster as he adapts. He will be fitted with several combinations of shoes until his trainer is satisfied that the perfect combination of shoes and toe weights has been hit upon—one that will promote an extended stride with perfect balance. A trotter's shoes weigh eight ounces or so, a pacer's about five.

In his early jogs, the horse develops his gait, gradually working up to faster times. If he seems ready for the track, the driver begins to extend him in four-mile jogs climaxed with a brief all-out burst of speed. As his times get faster, the workouts are reduced to two a week. By the day of his first real race he will have logged about 700 miles.

Each day at a harness track is a lesson in how to win races. It begins at sun-up, when the trainer arrives to check his horses. With assistant and stable hands, the day is planned out. They spend the morning working out the horses and the afternoon in such jobs as shoeing their runners and sizing up the competition.

If post-time for the first race is 8:30 P.M., the horses in the first race are on the track at 6:30 to begin the warm-up process. Three times in these two hours each horse will be jogged, then returned to the paddock for sponging and cooling out. First jog is in light harness and covers five miles, half of that distance at speed. Again, after a half-hour interval, the horse returns and makes some practice starts, finishing off with a mile run at a good clip. In his last appearance before the race, the horse runs another mile at a little less than all-out speed. This is about 40 minutes before his race. (Between races, the track is constantly in use by horses making their practice runs.)

In this elaborate warm-up procedure, the horse is worked for several miles even before he is called upon to give his all. Strenuous as it seems, the trotter or pacer needs this loosening in order to run in top form. He is still limbering up in the last moments before being summoned to the starting gate.

A HARNESS RACE

Harness tracks are usually a half-mile or five-eighths of a mile long. A few are mile-long ovals. Surfaces are firm, in contrast to the soft tracks of flat racing.

To begin a race, horses are guided into their positions side by side along the automobile-mounted starting gate. To effect a running start, the car moves down the track at a gradually increasing rate of speed, sulkies moving in line behind it. As the starting post is reached, the car speeds ahead and to one side. The wing-like gates fold away to clear the field.

The race is likely to be for the mile distance, although odd distances up to two miles are sometimes run. The driver should be a master tactician, keeping every move of his horse in tight control. On the longer oval of a mile track, he may attempt a pass on the turn, and he takes advantage of the longer straightaways. If he has been lucky enough to draw a place near the rail in the pre-race draw for starting position, he should be able to pull well ahead in the field at the outset of the race, when all runners move in toward the rail.

As one post after another is passed, the driver waits for the right moment to make his move for the lead. If he has been clever, he won't find his four-foot-wide sulky boxed in when the time comes, for if he cuts in, crowds, or collides with another sulky he will be penalized. He should know just how much he can ask of his horse. Two bursts of top speed are about all the average horse can deliver. The wise driver knows just when to "use" his horse. If the animal performs and finishes first, it takes only a few minutes for the judges and film replay to confirm that he has won a fairly run race.

7 | Color Types of the West

ORIGINS OF THE INDIAN PONY

Horses like the Mustang, the Appaloosa, and the Paint are often put in the catch-all category of "Indian ponies." Their story is a fascinating chapter in the history of the horse in America. It begins with the arrival in the New World of the Spanish explorers. The horses they brought with them were perhaps the finest of their time and the first to walk the continent since *Equus*, the ancestor of all horses, disappeared from it 10,000 years before.

Over the centuries breeders on the Iberian peninsula had produced excellent results from available strains. As early as the fifth century B.C., an important breed called Vilana had been developed by crossing native stock with the cold-blooded Northern horses of Celt invaders. In the third century B.C., the Vilanas were bred to Eastern stallions brought by the army of Carthage on its roundabout way to Rome. A horse of extraordinary speed and substance resulted. Many centuries later, when the Moors conquered Spain, they brought their culture and their splendid desert horses with them. With this infusion of Eastern blood, the Spanish horses moved another step closer to perfection. The mounts of the Spanish conquistadores and explorers were mostly Andalusian-bred and strong in the blood of the Barbary (Moroccan) horse. Thus the type of horse that debarked on the shores of the New World was in general very fine, the result of centuries of intelligent breeding. These were the horses—whether strayed, stolen, or bartered—that came into the possession of the American Indians. The "Indian pony," product of indiscriminate mating and the harsh plains environment, is their direct descendant.

Preceding pages: Western ponies forage on Colorado mountainside. Right: Horses being hoisted aboard ship for voyage to New World.

Embarcadero de los Cavallos,

The Indians took little time to get over their initial awe of the horse. During the 17th century many of the Southwestern tribes built up sizable herds and their braves learned to ride with fantastic skill. The horse provided greater range for tribal bands; it allowed hunters to kill single buffalo instead of stampeding herds into pit traps; and it made the Indian brave armed with bow and arrow fearsome in war.

One of the few Indian tribes to breed horses selectively was the Nez Perce of northern Idaho and northeastern Oregon. Meriwether Lewis described its horses as "an excellent race . . . eligantly formed, active and durable; many of them look like fine English coursers." These were the root stock of what is today called the Appaloosa breed. The Cayuse tribe also bred good horses. Environment was a

Top: Pawnee brave
breaking wild horse, as sketched
by George Catlin. Right:
Appaloosa mare and foal on Idaho range.

factor, since both these tribes lived in a mountainous region where the animals had good forage. On the Plains, the Indian ponies tended to be, as the artist George Catlin noted of the Comanche herd, "generally small, of the wild breed, tough and serviceable." Unlike the Cayuse and Nez Perce tribes, which selected both mares and stallions and gelded unsuitable males, the Plains tribes usually allowed their horses to mate freely.

Horsemen of today are trying to classify and improve the distinct types of Western horses by crossing with breeds of highly uniform and desirable characteristics, particularly the Thoroughbred and Arabian. For the present it is the coloration of the Appaloosa, the Pinto, and the Palomino that differentiates them. Conformation within each breed is still highly variable, but in time standards will be established.

APPALOOSA

Chief Joseph and his Nez Perce tribe were subjugated by the Government in 1877, after a long retreat from their home territory. The breeders of the Appaloosa had taken flight with about 2,000 of their excellent horses. Some 900 of the animals drowned in the fording of the Snake River and those remaining were taken by the Army and eventually sold off. Appaloosas left behind on the range were acquired by settlers or turned wild.

What saved the Appaloosa as a breed was its spotted hide, a feature valued by circuses and Wild West shows. A few breeders continued to produce Appaloosas to meet this demand, but, until 1936, the breed was always dangerously close to dissolution. In that year, Dr. Francis Haines, authority on the breed, published an article, "The Appaloosa or Palouse Horse," which attracted wide attention. In 1937 the Appaloosa Horse Club was formed. Its membership passed the 30,000 mark in 1971.

Tracing the origin of the breed is a continuing project of the club. As reported in its 72-page monthly magazine, evidence of spotted forebears of the Appaloosa has been found in the art of ancient China, in the epic literature of Korea, Japan, India, and Persia, and in Etruscan artifacts. Spotted horses were common in Britain in the 15th century.

Appaloosa conformation should be rugged, short-coupled, and not less that 14 hands in height. Color standards are more explicit: The eye must be encircled by white; skin must be mottled in any of a number of acceptable patterns, but especially about the nostrils; hoofs should have vertical dark and light bands.

Appaloosa clears
jump easily for young rider.
Breed is a consistent
favorite of Western horsemen.

Right: Pinto mares grazing in field of Arizona wildflowers. Opposite: Well-formed Pinto stallion of *tobiano* type.

PINTO

Favorite horse of the Comanche tribe was the Paint or Pinto (from the Spanish *pintado*). The Comanches were the buffalo hunters of the Great Plains, unsurpassed in horsemanship, and the Pinto—a fast, agile, and durable plains pony—was the ideal mount for running buffalo. Its coloration, too, pleased the Comanche braves; in fact, if a horse's markings were not bold enough, it might be touched up with paint or dye. When cattle raising spread over the Great Plains, the talents of the Pinto, as well as its stylish looks, were much in demand by cowboys. The Paint cow pony might bring $50 more than a solid-color horse of comparable quality.

Pinto horses are in the process of becoming established as a breed. Color is the standard that defines these horses, though, of course, to be registered an individual must also have sound conformation. The ideal pattern is 50/50 between

white and some other color; the minimum amount of marking acceptable in a horse with just one spot is an area equal to 75 square inches and this must be visible when the horse is standing normally. Pintos are described as *overo* or *tobiano*. *Overo* horses are marked with white on a basically colored coat; tail and mane are dark or mixed. A *tobiano* horse is basically white with markings in a darker color; mane and tail are the same color as neck and rump. The distinctive coloration of the Pinto is the result of a genetic strain that causes white areas combined with red or black areas on the skin. It reproduces consistently. Breeders believe this strain is an ancient one, citing the Pintos painted more than 3,000 years ago on the walls of Egyptian tombs. Now, after many decades of neglect, the breed is getting plenty of attention. Like the Appaloosa in the Sixties, it seems ready to "take off."

PALOMINO

With golden coat, flaxen mane and tail, and a glamorous past, the Palomino is a stylish and popular Western horse. Actually, it is still an unsettled question whether the Palomino can be called a true breed, since horses of its characteristic coloration often occur by accident in other families of horses. Also, breeding to get a Palomino foal is not a simple matter. The most reliable practice is to mate a Palomino to a light-chestnut animal of strong Eastern blood, rather than to another Palomino. Some horsemen are content to call the Palomino a breed, maintaining that the genes have come down over the centuries from a pure strain of golden horse, such as the ones seen in the Bayeux Tapestry, which records the invasion of England in 1066 by the Normans.

The Palomino Horse Registry accepts horses that meet its standards of coloration. Coat must be the color of a newly minted gold coin—not more than three shades darker, nor more than three shades lighter. Hairs of mane and tail must be at least 85 percent white. Face and legs may have white markings, but the rest of the body must be a golden color. The Registry groups Palominos into divisions according to the breed that is strongest in the background of an individual animal. These divisions include Thoroughbred, Arabian, Saddle Horse, Tennessee Walking Horse, Morgan, and Quarter Horse. The Quarter Horse bloodlines have produced the highest proportion of Palominos and many of the best performers, including the famous champion cutting horse, Cutter Bill.

The precise history of the Palomino in America is still being searched out. The name seems to have been in general

82

Spirited Palomino
in rodeo performance
with entertainer
and horseman Jimmy Dean.

use only about 60 years and probably derives from the name of some early owner who perhaps took a special interest in these horses. Chief Quanah Parker of the Comanches appears with one in an interesting photograph of the 1870's. Today no Western parade is complete without its phalanx of Palominos in full Western trappings. Though registrations have declined seriously from the high reached in 1947, the splendid Palomino will always have a place in the Western scene.

8 | Heavy Horses

Heavy horses may be seen today at state fairs, in events such as breed judging and weight-pulling contests. They still pull plows on many farms. But at the time of their development, in the Middle Ages, heavy horses were primarily instruments of war, functioning somewhat as tanks do in modern war. Of tremendous size, and weighing perhaps a ton or more, they plowed into battle bearing the weight of their own armor plus that of an armed and armored rider. The "Great Horse" of feudal combat was an animal of majestic appearance and awesome power; he was also scandalously pampered by his knightly owner.

Ancient ancestor of the Great Horse was *Equus robustus*, a large and powerful type native to Europe. From this stock, early medieval breeders produced the Flemish horse, which became the basis for later heavy-horse breeds; its closest counterpart today is the Belgian horse. The French used the Belgian horse as root of their Norman horse and from

Team of powerful
draft horses appears in
detail of painting
"Horse Fair" by Rosa Bonheur.

this breeding developed draft breeds including the Shire, Suffolk, and Clydesdale.

Heavy horses did more than carry knights in the Middle Ages. They also pulled the heavy, unsprung carriages of the time over the rough roads of Europe and Britain, and gradually they supplanted oxen for farm use.

After gunpowder revolutionized warfare in the 17th century, heavy horses carried on in peaceful tasks. In the United States they supplied power for the tremendous agricultural expansion of the 19th century.

Twentieth-century mechanization has largely deprived the strong and willing drafters of their usefulness, and their numbers have declined greatly. Yet the continuance of these breeds seems assured, thanks to horsemen who value their ancient lineage and heroic proportions.

86

Flaxen mane and white blaze on face are typical of Belgians, as seen in this group of mares and foals.

BELGIAN

Belgian horsemen bred this giant with great care for purity of standards. It descends from the ancient Flemish horse and is thought to have no Eastern blood at all. A late starter in the United States—it was first imported in 1886—its registrations are now about double those of any other breed.

The Belgian is the heaviest of the draft horses, attaining a weight between 1,900 and 2,200 pounds. It is not, however, the tallest. It is extremely "drafty" in appearance—blocky, close-coupled, with short, powerful legs, wide girth, and massive neck. Chestnut, roan, and sorrel are the usual and most acceptable colors, frequently with flaxen mane and white-blazed face. Belgians are placid and easily maintained.

SHIRE

At 17 hands and taller, the Shire is the tallest of the heavy-horse breeds. It was developed in England, no doubt with important contributions from the Norman horse introduced by William the Conqueror in 1066. Its uses were mainly agricultural.

The Shire is almost as heavy as the Belgian, but longer-backed and less rotund. It is called a "feather-legged" breed because of the flowing hairs that grow about the fetlocks of all four legs. Black, bay, and brown are the common colors. Legs are white from knee or hock to hoof, and the face often has white markings.

In the 1880's Shires had a spurt of popularity in the United States with 400 imported in the year 1887 alone. Registrations subsequently fell off sharply.

SUFFOLK

While many of the draft breeds have cut a figure in city settings—before heavy carriages or merchants' wagons—the Suffolk has always been a farm type valued for its willingness and ease of handling. Its physical characteristics are highly distinct. Smallest of the heavy horses at between 15:2 and 16:2 hands, it is quite rotund and drafty looking. The Suffolk is always chestnut color, with little if any white.

The history of this draft breed is unique in that it apparently descends from one prepotent stallion. This was the Crisp horse of Ufford, foaled in 1768.

There was little demand for Suffolks in the United States, where horses of similar size could be had from native stock. Many were exported to Canada, but a total of only about 3,000 have been registered in the U.S.

CLYDESDALE

A heavy horse and a graceful one is the Clydesdale. It moves with the kind of style and action characteristic of the hot-blooded breeds. Conformation in part accounts for this. It is unusually clean-legged for a draft breed, with muscular thighs and large feet that give stability and balance to its underpinnings. Its pasterns are long and flexible, and though it is tall—between 16 and 17 hands—it is the lightest of the drafters.

In the show ring the Clydesdale is responsive, high-stepping, even flamboyant due to the long, silky feathers that flow about its fetlocks; it moves along smartly without being urged with touches of the whip. Clydesdale colors are brown or bay, often with splashes of white on the face and legs.

The breed, named after the River Clyde in Scotland, is hardly more than a century old. It prospered through its Scottish breeders' strict attention to quality and pedigree. The Clyde stallion Dunure Footprint, foaled in 1908, must be ranked with the great equine progenitors of all time, based on the number and superiority of his offspring.

In America, the Clydesdale was considered the most desirable breed for city hauling. Anyone who has ever seen the splendid matched team maintained by the Anheuser-Busch brewing company can tell why. For power coupled with elegance, the Clyde's only rival is the Percheron. Canada supplied America with its first Clydesdales, but direct importation from Scotland was going strong by the 1870's. Today only the Belgian is more popular.

Clydesdale stallion
shows breed's feathered fetlocks.
"Roman" nose is characteristic
of draft horses in general.

Ideal Percheron (below)
combines strength and refinement.
Right: Willing team on Indiana farm.

PERCHERON

In the great days of the drafters, this breed was considered the aristocrat of them all. A farmer putting his Percherons to the plow might reflect that this same breed once pulled the carriages of the Bourbon kings of France. They were durable, docile, prompt, and they were good sires. The get of a Percheron stallion was likely to be of good quality, even out of a mare that was only average. Percherons were so much in demand that businessmen bought them as investments. At one time there were more registered in the U.S. than any other breed; total registration is about 250,000.

The horse that so caught the fancy of America originated in the northwestern region of France called La Perche. A descendant of the Flemish horse, it received in medieval times an infusion of desert blood from horses captured during

90

the Moorish invasion of Europe. Arabian influences show in the Percheron's smooth conformation and in its hardy nature. The head, too, has more refinement than is usual with other draft breeds. Nine out of ten Percherons are gray or black (the lighter color was preferred for coach horses as being more visible at night). At 1,900 to 2,200 pounds, the Percheron outweighs the Clydesdale and Suffolk, but it is shorter than the Belgian or Shire, at 16 to 16:3 hands.

Finest of all Percheron sires in the U.S. was Laet, foaled in 1915. His many Grand Champion sons and daughters dominated the major shows of the Twenties and early Thirties. Such a sire is called a "breed builder."

In breeding horses for hunting, it is common for a Percheron to be crossed with a Thoroughbred to get an animal of stamina and substance.

91

9|Native American Breeds

In the 400-odd years since horses made their reappearance in America as mounts of the Spanish explorers, four new major breeds have originated that are strictly American natives. They are the Morgan—bred in New England; the American Saddle Horse and the Tennessee Walking Horse—whose origins go back to the plantations of the Old South; and the harness-racing Standardbred (see Chapter 6).

Preceding pages: Pair of
Morgans performs in coaching event.
Above: Well-matched
Morgan team is judged at show.

THE MORGAN HORSE

In the mid-1790's, a Vermonter named Justin Morgan acquired a two-year-old stallion of promising ancestry, a smallish horse, about 14 hands high, that weighed perhaps 900 pounds. Its look was distinctive—part Arabian, part Dutch light-draft horse, with a short back, short, muscular legs, a thick barrel, massive shoulders, and a fine head.

95

Morgan's compact bay was a versatile performer: mighty at moving stumps, rocks, and logs; unbeatable in quarter-mile sprints in harness or under saddle; fast-stepping and stylish on the road. And he was noted for his patient and willing disposition.

The ancestry of "Justin Morgan's horse" is not known for certain. A relative of Morgan supported the claim of some that the horse's sire was a famous racing stallion, once the war charger of a British officer, named True Briton (also Beautiful Bay). Others say that the horse Justin Morgan was sired by a Dutch-bred horse named Young Bulrock. Mr. Morgan, it was said by his son, called the bay stallion a "Dutch horse." His dam was supposed to have been of the strain begun by an imported stallion named Wildair that was part Thoroughbred and part Arabian. The Morgan Horse Register opts for True Briton and the Wildair mare as parents of Justin Morgan and puts the year of his birth at 1789.

The stallion Justin Morgan is perhaps the best-known sire that has ever lived. He is the direct ancestor of all Morgan horses and his characteristics have reproduced faithfully from generation to generation. The quality of his get began to be noticed after he died at age 29. The establishment of the Morgan breed came about largely through three of his sons—Sherman, Bulrush, and Woodbury—each of whom founded a family over many years of standing at stud in New England towns. The Sherman strain was outstanding for speed. Sherman's son Black Hawk was champion trotter of his day, supposedly unbeaten; he became founder of a subfamily, the Black Hawks. Ethan Allan, a son of Black Hawk, was named trotting Champion of the World in 1853.

By the 1850's, Morgans were in great demand, and Vermont was their foremost producer. In the Civil War they proved fully as serviceable as the excellent Thoroughbred cavalry mounts of the Confederate army. Fortunately, after the war the Army continued to propagate the breed for cavalry use. The Morgans' rank in the trotting world slipped,

Morgan horse is low and compact. Powerful, arching neck and lofty carriage of the head are characteristic.

however, as Standardbreds began setting the records. But the Morgan remained a standby for farm, ranch, and road work.

In the later 1800's, the integrity of the Morgan as a breed was threatened by interbreeding with Standardbreds for the sake of giving the Morgan added speed. As yet no registry existed, although a book, *Morgan Horses* by D. C. Linsley, published in 1857, had traced the development of the breed. The *Morgan Horse and Register* finally appeared at the turn of the century, due to the efforts of Colonel Joseph Battell of Middlebury, Vermont, who had studied the breed for many years and had even given the Government a farm in Vermont for the breeding and improving of Morgan horses (run since 1951 by the University of Vermont).

In the rivalry between horse and automobile that enlivened the early 1900's, the Morgan, like other breeds, lost ground. Among its faithful supporters were Charles A. Stone and his son Whitney, who kept the register going. Following World War II, Morgans began their comeback. The current annual number of about 1,500 registrations is much more heartening than the 75 or so being registered yearly in the late 1920's.

Today's Morgan has left behind some of the draft-horse style of Mr. Morgan's prepotent stallion, but the basic character is there. This horse is still muscular and compact at between 14 and 15 hands, still long-lived and of friendly, generous disposition. Bays, browns, and blacks are the colors usually seen, with an occasional chestnut. The breed can be seen at its best at the Morgan Horse Show held each year in Northampton, Massachusetts.

98

Morgan is bred as ideal
all-purpose horse. Mare and foal
above are on breeding farm in
Vermont, home state of Justin Morgan.

AMERICAN SADDLE HORSE

The American Saddle Horse is primarily a show-ring animal. Originally bred to be a stylish and comfortable plantation walker, it is now educated to give an extremely mannered performance under saddle, an exhibition unrivaled for power, elegance, and beauty. Flashing into the ring, the Saddle Horse is a breathtaking study in equine excitability held by the rider in perfect control.

American Saddle Horses are trained as either three-gaited or five-gaited performers. Both types do the walk, trot, and canter; the five-gaited animals have, besides these natural gaits, two acquired ones—a slow gait and the rack. In whatever step he moves, the action of the Saddle Horse is alert, smooth, and showy, with phenomenal elevation of the feet. His canter, for example, is not the free, ground-covering motion of other horses, but an extremely "collected," or reined-in rocking action. The rack is a spectacular four-beat gait in which the horse bursts ahead at speeds sometimes approaching 30 miles an hour, but with the same precisely-cadenced footwork and high elevation of the feet displayed in all the other gaits.

To become a five-gaited Saddler, an individual of the breed needs an aptitude for the two unnatural gaits. Due to the extra muscular exertion that they require, he will develop into a somewhat more powerful-looking animal than his three-gaited relative.

Not all members of the breed are shown under saddle. Some are trained to perform in fine harness, drawing a four-wheeled show wagon at the walk and park trot.

In conformation, the Saddle Horse averages close to 16

100

American Saddle
Horse steps out for
Earl Teater,
master trainer of Saddlers.

101

102

Saddler's fetlocks flex
sharply, as seen
in action of well-handled
show contestant above.

hands. He is rounded and muscular, since his high-stepping action requires great strength and control. Sloping shoulders contribute to the smoothness of his movement. His back is short, ending in a flattish croup. His handsome head is carried very high and proudly. Saddle Horse colors run to brown, black, bay, or chestnut, often with a flash of white on the face and legs. The pasterns of the Saddler's leg are unusually long, and it is these, flexing sharply at every step, that give this horse his exceptional style in moving.

The beauty of the Saddle Horse show performer is partly inborn, partly man-made. His coat has been brought to a lustrous sheen by hours of brushing. His long silky tail and its plume-like set are also the result of cosmetic attention, including hand-combing and perhaps the addition of false hair. Also, the muscle that normally acts to lower the tail has been surgically nicked, causing the base of the tail to rise in a spirited arch. (This applies to the five-gaited horses; three-gaited Saddlers are customarily shown with natural tails shaved along the top of the bone.) Specially-weighted shoes are one of the assists the Saddle Horse has in achieving perfectly balanced action.

When a Saddle Horse performs with spirit, precision, and instant response, it is testimony first to the training he has received, and second to the quality of his ancestors. One of the first great horses to contribute to the breed was a Canadian pacer, Tom Hal, foaled in 1806. In his 41-year lifetime he founded a strain of Saddlers of extraordinary quality. In 1839 the foundation sire of the American Saddle Horse breed was foaled, a Thoroughbred named Denmark. He became a racing great, and in 1851, in a mating with a Saddler called

the "Stevenson mare," produced a son who later surpassed him in greatness, Gaines Denmark. It is from Gaines Denmark (who won fame also as a Civil War charger) that most horses of the breed descend.

Top performers in this century have been Bourbon King, from the family of Tom Hal, and the magnificent Wing Commander, supreme among five-gaited Saddlers between 1948 and 1954.

For a Saddler of such championship promise, the price may go to $70,000 or more. But the Saddler is not such a rarified creature as all this expense and attention suggest. Strong, quick to learn, and basically good-natured, a Saddler in retirement from the ring, or one of insufficient promise to be trained for show, makes a spirited mount for pleasure riding. Some have excelled as hunters.

104

The great Wing Commander (Earl Teater riding) exhibits form that earned 200 championships in nine years of Saddle Horse show competition.

TENNESSEE WALKING HORSE

In 1935, just yesterday as breeds go, the official registry of the Tennessee Walking Horse Breeder's Association was formed. Sixty thousand entries have been made since then, a phenomenal show of popularity by the horse some call "the gentleman of equines." The specialty of this breed is the running walk, a gait so smooth that it's possible for a rider to hold a glass of water without spilling a drop. But probably it is the Tennessee Walker's temperament that has earned him so many friends throughout the U.S. Patient and amiable, he is the safe choice for the small home stable, especially where chores such as feeding and grooming are to be done by a youngster. Sure-footed and incredibly comfortable to ride, he is an ideal mount, too, for trail riding.

The American Saddle Horse and the Tennessee Walking Horse had similar origins and retain many points of similarity. However, the Walker has acquired his own distinct characteristics. Standing between 15 and 16 hands and weighing up to 1,200 pounds, his broad chest, rounded barrel, muscular shoulders and quarters, and strong bones bespeak an animal of both style and substance. The neck is shorter than the Saddler's and not so haughtily arched. The head, if not classic, is broad-skulled, with a sensitive, worldly-wise expression that results from the breed's characteristic eye, which has a sloping and wrinkled upper lid. The color range is broad; Walkers may be either black (the most desirable color for show), chestnut, roan, white, brown, bay, gray, or gold. Most have some white markings; the roans are sometimes well splashed with white.

GAITS

Tennessee Walking Horses are three-gaited, moving at a walk, running walk, and canter. Though supremely comfortable in all three, it is the running walk for which the horse is most highly valued. The pleasure Walker glides along in this four-beat gait at perhaps eight miles an hour. Show Walkers are trained for greater speed. Analyzing the gait, one sees that each foot moves independently. The forward reach of the forefeet is extreme, and the placement of the hind feet may overreach the forefeet at their rearmost point in the stride by a foot or more. There is not the slightest seesaw motion in the back; the horse holds it horizontal but has to make a muscular compensation for this by pumping his head up and down as he moves. Due to the effort of the gait, the horse develops a very strong neck and forequarters.

Note long forward reach
of rear foot in
ground-covering stride
of Tennessee Walking Horse.

HISTORY

Tennessee Walking Horses developed over a period of about a century and a half, mainly in the Middle Basin of Tennessee. The horses that carried settlers into this region from Virginia and the Carolinas were mostly pacers of Canadian and Narragansett bloodlines. Easy-gaited and sure-footed, they were ideal for plantation and road work. With these animals as base stock, Tennessee breeders worked toward developing a type of horse with a loose and speedy walk. The lush country, with its rich mineral soil, favored the breeding of fine horses. Crosses were made with many breeds: Arabian, Thoroughbred, Morgan, and the closely-related Saddle Horse. By the 1880's, the distinguishing characteristic of the "plantation walkers"—their running walk—was fixed. Their appearance, however, remained highly variable. The horse that would change this situation was foaled in 1886 in Lexington, Kentucky. This was Black Allan, a horse of first-rate bloodlines, who had failed as both trotter and pacer because of his peculiar loose stride. At age 17, his possibilities as a sire were recognized by Mr. James Brantly of Manchester, Tennessee, who bought Black Allan and bred him to his excellent Walking mare, Gertrude. The get of this mating was Roan Allen, a truly great horse, a peerless seven-gaited show performer, and ancestor of top show horses. Black Allan sired many other famous Walkers and in 1935 was named first foundation sire of the breed. As his descendants multiplied, the characteristics of the breed were stabilized.

One of the largest horse shows in the country is the Walking Horse "Celebration," held yearly in Shelbyville, Tennessee.

107

10│The Quarter Horse

The development of the Quarter Horse began in America before the Revolution. Now, with a total of nearly one million registered, it is the most numerous breed in the U.S.

Typically, today's Quarter Horse stands about 15 hands, has a compact barrel, broad, muscular shoulders and haunches, and a handsome, breedy head that is carried rather forward in workmanlike fashion. The withers are lower to the ground than the croup. The overall look is low, close-coupled, powerful, and heavily weighted up front.

The popularity of the Quarter Horse is well deserved. It is intelligent, willing, at ease in the company of people and other animals, and easy to keep. Whether as a short-distance racer, a cow pony, or a dazzling rodeo performer, it's in the nature of the Quarter Horse to give its all. Certainly, the machine that might equal it for working cattle is unlikely ever to be invented.

HISTORY

The so-called Chickasaw horse was an important influence in the development of the Quarter Horse. In the 16th century, when the Spanish expeditionary forces of DeSoto and others were exploring the area of what is now Florida, South Carolina, and Georgia, they lost many of their excellent mounts to hostile Indians, especially to the Chickasaws. Mating freely with the Indians' stock, the Spanish horses transmitted their desert-blooded characteristics and there developed a desirable strain of small, agile horse that came to be called the Chickasaw.

Southern colonists, seeing possibilities in these compact, speedy animals, mated them with horses of generally Euro-

110

pean ancestry and developed a low, muscular sprinter which they ran in quarter-mile races. Known as the Quarter-Pather, or the Colonial Quarter-of-a-Mile Running Horse, this was the prototype of today's Quarter Horse. Before the racing ascendancy of the Thoroughbred, the Quarter-Pathers roused great sporting excitement on the "Race Streets" of villages and towns. There is an account of one quarter-mile race in colonial times for which the winnings amounted to more than $40,000 in gold, silver, and goods.

Subsequent breeding of these racers preserved the characteristic that made their sudden burst of speed possible: frontal weight which reduced a horse's tendency to rise up on pushing off to a start.

Preceding pages: Quarter Horse makes
fast getaway in pursuit of
scampering steer. Above: Barrel racer
wheels mount into next leg of course.

GREAT SIRES

Janus, a horse of Eastern descent imported to America in 1752, was the single most influential stallion in the development of the Quarter Horse. One of the great sires in American equine history, he was not a Thoroughbred in the strict sense, for he was born before the early foals of Matchem, first foundation sire of the Thoroughbred breed. But he was a strong and illustrious racer, more than equal to the grueling four-mile heats customary in his day. To his offspring he passed on a gift for early speed. His own conformation—low, muscular, and rounded—became char-

112

Crossbreeding with Thoroughbreds has given Quarter Horse racer rangier conformation than stock-horse type.

acteristic of the Quarter Horse breed.

Of modern sires, the most famous is King, who died in 1958. Unlike his father, Zanaton—a racer described as the "Mexican Man o' War"—King's fame was earned as a sire. His splendid bloodlines have shown in the number and quality of his foals; a high percentage of them have been champion racers, show performers, and cutting horses. One of King's daughters, a racer named Squaw H, was never beaten over the quarter-mile. Most famous of his sons is Poco Bueno, one of the savviest cutting horses of all time and sire of a line of champion stock horses.

113

Left: Quarter Horses as circus performers. Bottom: Quarter Horse cow pony is durable, willing, adept with cattle.

BREEDING

So varied are the talents of the Quarter Horse that breeders have differed as to which characteristics should be emphasized. Conformation breeders have sought to preserve the traditional low and heavy structure. Breeders of the horse for stock work have wanted less beefiness and more agility. At one time, this latter group formed under the name National Quarter Horse Association, as separate from the American Quarter Horse Association founded in 1940. The two have since joined.

A third school of thought has been that of the racing enthusiasts, whose concern is for speed. To obtain it they have bred plenty of Thoroughbred blood into the Quarter Horse racer, bringing it quite close in conformation to the Thoroughbred type. This group of breeders now forms the very important and active Racing Division of the American Quarter Horse Association.

Thus, in conformation, the Quarter Horse may be either the rangy type possessing speed, or the short, muscular type of animal able to win a tug-of-war with a steer.

RACING

In 1949, crowds at the Bay Meadows race track in San Mateo, California, were introduced to Quarter Horse races as preliminary events to the running of the Thoroughbreds. Purses were only a few hundred dollars and distances were 330 to 440 yards. But the brief, blistering runs and the photo-finishes were a new kind of excitement to most racing fans, and the sport quickly caught on: Contrast the 8,722 recognized Quarter Horse races run in 1972 with the 25 recognized in 1945. The total of purses in 1972 was $13,578,188. In fact, the richest purse in all racing has for years gone to the winner of a Quarter Horse event, the All American Futurity. In 1973, it was $1,000,000. For a horse of All American caliber, purchase price may exceed $120,000.

Thrilling finishes, the feature that has given Quarter Horse racing its great success, are guaranteed by a tightly organized system of classification. Each horse is graded according to its track time and is placed in a division with horses of similar speed. First rank classification is AAA, for which qualifying times are 12.1 seconds for 220 yards, 13.6 for 250, 15.9 for 300, 17.3 for 330, 18.3 for 350, 20.6 for 400, and 22.5 for 440. Divisions continue through AA, A, and on to the lowest—D—where comparable times are 13.1 seconds for 220 yards, and 24.2 seconds for 440 yards.

Foremost among the great sires of modern Quarter Horse racers was Three Bars, a Thoroughbred once bought for $300 and later given away. It was at stud that Three Bars proved his worth, siring several hundred foals whose accumulated earnings have exceeded three million dollars.

Even matching of
runners is key to exciting
close finishes in
sport of Quarter Horse racing.

STOCK WORK

For working with stock, the horse the cowhands rank first is the Quarter Horse. It has "cow savvy"—an instinct for outguessing and outmaneuvering a steer on the run. Like any other animal, the Quarter Horse has to be trained for its work, but it is willing to learn and can develop an uncanny ability. Its talent may well be inherited from its hot-blooded ancestors, horses that were used by Mediterranean peoples and by the American Indians not only for herding but for bull-baiting and buffalo-running as well.

The Quarter Horse is masterful in every phase of stock work—roping, bulldogging, and cutting. But it is in cutting—separating an animal from the herd—that a Quarter Horse really demonstrates wizardry; this is often a main attraction in rodeos and Western shows. Once the cow to be cut from

Good Quarter Horse
knows his part in calf
roping, performs
with nimbleness and know-how.

the herd has been indicated, the horse works on his own without direction from his rider. He has learned to keep the position of advantage over a cow. As it breaks away, he heads it off with a burst of speed; as it reverses or feints, he digs in to a dead stop, pivots, and lunges forward to turn the cow onto another tack. If the cow makes a run, he calculates the perfect drift for intercepting it. It is an extraordinary display of equine agility.

The training of such a horse is usually completed by the time he is four or five years old. It may begin when he is as young as three weeks. One very successful trainer begins with a horse four years of age and completes its training in one year. So there is no rigid procedure in the making of a Quarter Horse cow pony. It all adds up to developing the animal's inborn knack.

119

11 | Ponies

Ponies are small horses that come in a great variety of sizes, conformations, and personalities. Some pony strains trace back to antiquity, while others are even now being developed by breeders. Though their size (14 hands and under) makes them suitable for children, they should never be pampered as pets. A pony thrives on a hardy life and — if possible—the company of its own kind.

WELSH PONY

In the U.S., the term Welsh pony means the Welsh Mountain pony, of which about 20,000 are registered. This admirable riding pony is distinct from its larger cart-horse cousin, the Welsh Cob.

Originally a wild native type, the Mountain pony was considerably refined by the introduction of Eastern blood some hundred years ago, when a number of Arabian stallions were turned out among Welsh mares. Today's Welsh is markedly Arabian in many points of conformation, especially the head, neck, and high-set tail. Its strong back is short and well-coupled, the loins broad and muscular. The legs are short and move with a flexible, elevated forward reach. The Welsh pony should be of a solid color. In the U.S. they are usually in the gray, white, or chestnut ranges. Fairly large, their official upper limit is 12:2 hands. They are easily maintained.

Fine-harness enthusiasts admire the Welsh's smart action, but the Welsh Pony Society of America prefers to emphasize the horse's excellent riding qualities. In the hunting field, especially, his spirit and relish for jumping are exceptional. Little wonder that registrations in the breed are gaining fast.

122

Preceding pages: Prize-winning harness pony. Right: Welsh pony shows Arabian influence in delicate ears, prominent cheeks, arching neck.

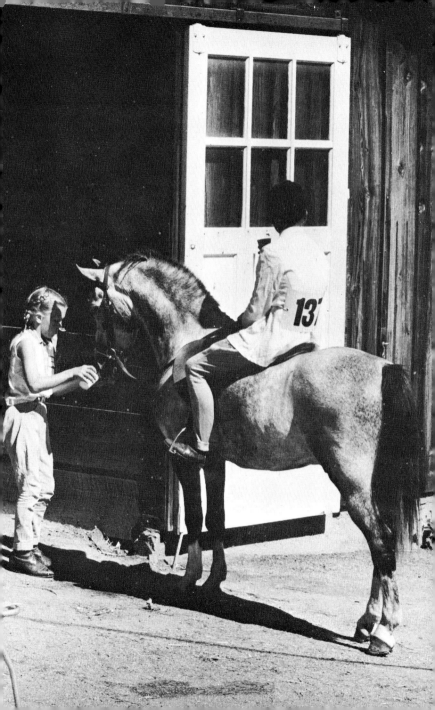

SHETLAND

The Sheltie, as the English call this sturdy pony, originated on the Shetland Islands off the coast of Scotland. It is the most popular of the pony breeds, with 80,000 registered by the American Shetland Pony Club.

There is evidence that the Shetland existed as early as 600 A.D. A Celtic stone carving from before the Norse invasions (c. 800 A.D.) shows similar small horses. Like all wild ponies, the Shetland is the product of its original environment. A rocky terrain made it sure-footed; a meager diet of heather, seaweed, and marsh grass inhibited its growth, and the cold sea wind brought about its thick coat, so long and furry in winter that it becomes a rainproof thatch. The domesticated Shetland thrives best on the barest essentials: hay or grass, water, and a simple shed for shelter in rough weather.

Today's purebred ranges from as small as 26 inches to the 46-inch limit set by the American Shetland Pony Club. A deep chest, heavily-muscled back, and round barrel are characteristic; legs are very short. The Island type, long used in the mines of the British Isles, looks like a miniature draft horse. The American type has been refined through selective breeding; its profile sometimes is dished in the Arabian manner. Shetland colors include mouse gray, black, bay, brown, chestnut, cream, white, spotted, and dapple. Shetlands excel in harness, and perform well in the growing sport of pony harness racing. They can be good jumpers, too. Pony jumping events are usually grouped by size. Ponies under 11:2 hands jump 2 feet; 11:2 to 13 hands jump 2 feet 6 inches; 13 to 14:2 jump 3 feet.

American Shetland (left)
is more refined than original
island type, which looks
like a draft horse in miniature.

HACKNEY

No pony works in harness with more style than the Hackney. It was developed from the Hackney horse of England, and its bloodlines trace back to those important stallions, the Darley Arabian, the Godolphin Barb, and the Byerly Turk.

Today, Hackney ponies outnumber the horses. They are fairly large, averaging 12 to 13 hands. Bay is the usual color, though black, brown, chestnut, even gray and roan, are seen.

Most owners would feel that to use the Hackney under saddle is to miss the point; fine harness is his forte. His bearing is proud, with arched neck and high tail, his look alert and eager, his action taut and elegant. So this is no mere child's mount, but a pony for those able to appreciate his spirit, flash, and very special breeding.

CONNEMARA

County Galway in Ireland is home of the gentle Connemara. Largest of the ponies, he serves dutifully and handsomely as a cart horse; in fact, this comes quite naturally to him, since the first foundation sire of the breed, a horse named Cannon Ball, was a famous trotter in his time. It is in the hunting field, however, that the Connemara is even more at home. Here he can use his often phenomenal jumping ability. (Unforgettable was the 54-inch Connemara, Little Squire, who for many years in the 1930's was a U.S. open jumping champion.)

In conformation and action, these ponies have the look of miniature Thoroughbreds. The registry limits height to 14:2 hands, but individuals sometimes outgrow this. Almost every other Connemara is gray, and blacks are frequent.

Top: Bold, stylish
Hackney pony takes a turn after
topping its class at show.
Left: Connemara is a willing jumper.

ICELANDIC PONY

Until recently Iceland restricted export of this little horse, but it is now a welcome addition to the pony roster in the U.S. It originated with stock brought to Iceland by the Norsemen around 865 A.D. and has served through the centuries on the farms of that island country. Icelanders (and hardy visitors) also use them as mounts in the sport of trekking (cross-country camping). They are tall, standing at an average 13:2 hands, and the characteristic colors are red and chestnut, or spotted chestnut. Hardy animals with friendly natures, their numbers will no doubt quickly increase in the United States.

DARTMOOR AND EXMOOR

From the moors of Devon and Somerset come two wild pony races, the Dartmoor and the Exmoor. They are small, about 12 hands, and resemble the Welsh pony, with strong signs of an ancient mingling with desert stock. Breeders have taken special interest in them recently since they are daring little jumpers and when crossed with full-size horses

Herd of Iceland's
sturdy, sure-footed ponies
grazes green tundra
of their native island.

produce good hunters. On coming in from the wild, however, they are quite rough and need firm training.

The Dartmoor is a stockier horse than the Exmoor. Colors of both include brown. bay, black, gray, and chestnut; purebreds are never spotted. The stride is a reaching one, without the showy elevation of the Welsh. These rugged and spirited ponies are fairly new to the American scene, but they will surely make a place for themselves.

NATIVE AMERICAN PONIES
In the United States there are several wild or crossbred pony strains. The four that follow are perhaps best known.

KENTUCKY SADDLE PONY
This is a cultivated strain produced by crossing a pony mare or stallion with an American Saddle Horse. The result is a Saddle Horse in small scale, and the ideal alternative to the Hackney pony for showing under saddle. Its spirited bearing, highly elevated step, and refined conformation very much resemble the well-bred Hackney. Many are five-gaited.

CHINCOTEAGUE PONY

Chincoteagues are a wild race found off the coast of Virginia on the islands of Assateague and Chincoteague. Marguerite Henry has given an account of them in her classic book for children, *Misty of Chincoteague*. A no-doubt related band roams the island of Okracoke off North Carolina. These island ponies are possibly descended from horses that survived the wreck of a Spanish ship in the 16th century. Over generations of grazing on tough marsh grasses, the animals diminished in size to their present range of 12:2 to 13 hands. Once a year they are rounded up and herded across the channel from Assateague to Chincoteague and the foals are put up for auction. They may be of any color, though a solid color is considered a sign of the desert blood of their supposed ancestors.

130

Top: Chincoteague mare and foal. Right: Marsh Tackys, another coastal pony strain, may be Thoroughbred descendants.

MARSH TACKY
Also in the Carolinas is another wild strain, the Marsh Tackys. They are a fairly refined type, and may—as the story goes—be descendants of Thoroughbreds that turned to the wild after the Civil War.

PONY OF THE AMERICAS
This ranks as a breed and has an official stud book. Its progenitors were a Shetland stallion and an Appaloosa mare, and it carries on the Appaloosa coloration, particularly the "varnish marks" (dark spots) about the nose, eyes, and mouth. When fully grown, they are permanently registered if they meet the requirement for height, between 11:2 and 13 hands. They have become popular cow ponies in the West.

12 | Fox Hunting

Followers of the hunt think little of its dangers; its satisfactions are too great. Once or twice weekly throughout a five-month season (between fall harvest and spring planting) they meet to ride after foxes at breakneck speed. The quarry is fast and clever, traditional courtesies are observed, and always there is the rider's thrill in taking a fine horse over whatever jumps may loom.

The development of the Thoroughbred breed made this modern form of hunting possible. Before the 18th century, woodland hunters after the stag, the boar, or the roe might amble along at two miles an hour, with an occasional stop for refreshment. Today's fox hunters are likely to ride for five hours and cover 40 miles, much taken at the gallop.

THE THOROUGHBRED HUNTER

"Hunter" is not a breed name. Any horse that performs creditably on the hunting field may be called a hunter, whether it be an Appaloosa or a Connemara pony. But "hunter" generally refers to an animal of the type specially bred and trained for fox hunting. The breed that dominates among hunters, due to its speed and incredible endurance, is the Thoroughbred.

The demands of the hunting field require certain qualities in the hunter not associated with the Thoroughbred as flat racer. The streamlined racer propels himself at great speed over a smooth course of less than two miles. The hunter performs as a jumper and a long-distance runner all day over difficult terrain. Full, hard muscling and sound bone give him "substance" to endure the punishment of the ride, perhaps under a heavy rider. He appears closer to

134

Preceding pages:
Riders assemble, as eager
hounds wait signal
for fox hunt to begin.

the ground than his flat-track brother, sturdier through the neck, shoulder, and barrel. (The hunter, of course, is a mature and fully developed horse, while the two- or three-year-old race horse is still a juvenile.)

The skeleton of the horse is its inner spring, and the hunter's is well designed for his function. Powerful hindquarters provide the lift he needs to sail over obstacles. Sloping shoulders absorb the shocks of landing. Prominent withers keep the saddle from slipping in the helter-skelter of the chase. During the long and careful training process, a hunter's leg bones are allowed the necessary time to "set," to become dense, hard, resistant to injury. When put to full use at age five, he is in condition for the worst kind of country. Whereas the hard-used racing Thoroughbred is often broken down at age five, the hunter is just beginning his career.

Good temper is another quality necessary for the hunter. A field member is no asset to the hunt on a horse that reacts excitedly, kicks at the hounds, refuses jumps, or is disobedient to commands. The animal's inborn disposition has much to do with his deportment, but training is equally important. If properly schooled, the spirited hunter learns to take the most awesome jumps fearlessly and to stay calm amidst the general excitement around him. He will show a knack for doing the sensible thing.

Crossbreeding of Thoroughbreds with cold-blooded horses is sometimes done to produce characteristics such as great size or heavy bone. Breeders in Ireland and England have gotten bold, hardy hunters out of crosses between Thoroughbreds and wild ponies.

HISTORY

Hunting on horseback is a sport of ancient age. Wherever horsemanship was cultivated in early civilizations, there were horsemen who turned the mundane matter of killing animals for food into something more exciting—a test of themselves and their horses.

It was in the Middle Ages that the modern form of the hunt began to evolve. It still bore resemblance to the hunts of antiquity. The game might be a boar or some other fierce animal, and to keep the flesh intact for the table the animal was dispatched with lances rather than by the dogs. Yet the ritual courtesies and standards of sportsmanship that mark today's hunt were already being established. An important step was the manual of the hunt written in the 14th century by the French Count Gaston de Foix (Gaston Phoebus), and later given to the English by the Duke of York in his book *The Master of Game*. In adopting the courtly French style of hunting, the English simply anglicized such field calls as *Ty a hillaut* (the game's afoot) into "Tally ho"; *illoeques* (here's the spot) into "Yoicks." First mention in print of a formally-conducted fox hunt is dated 1581, during the reign of Henry VIII. In the 1600's the number of people riding to hounds in England was swelled by the addition of men and women from the prosperous middle class.

The 18th century saw fox hunting established in America, largely in Maryland, Virginia, and Massachusetts. New Jersey and Pennsylvania also initiated hunts that have become venerable traditions. In fact, fox hunting has taken hold in almost every state where topography allows it and where people have the time and wherewithal to pursue it.

Light but durable Thoroughbreds turned fox hunting into sport of fast-paced pursuit.

HUNT TERMS

Blank, to draw blank: to fail to find a fox.

Cast or **Draw a covert:** to search for the scent, hounds casting on their own or directed by the huntsman.

Cry or **Give tongue:** the baying of a fox hound.

Earth: a hole of any kind where the fox can hide.

Heads up: hounds that have lost the scent lift their heads while trying to find it again.

Hit off the line: when hounds regain the scent.

Line: the trail of the fox.

Loss: pack is "at loss" when it cannot stay on the scent.

Mask: face of the fox.

Mob: action of the pack in killing the fox before it has a chance to run.

Pink: scarlet coats worn by many hunt members, called "pinks" after a London tailor of that name.

Ride straight: to jump obstacles as they come.

Riot: hounds are said to riot when they run after game other than the fox.

Scent: smell of the fox, by which it is trailed by the pack.

Stern: the tail of a hound.

HUNT OFFICIALS

Master of Fox Hounds is the man (or woman) who has charge of both the season's sport and the social aspects of the hunt. (Some 121 hunts are currently active, according to the Masters of Fox Hounds Association of America.) The M.F.H. is a person respected for his hunting skill and his diplomacy in dealing with field members, professional huntsmen, and property owners. He is responsible for maintaining a good pack of hounds and for planning and presiding over successful days afield. On a hunt the M.F.H. may also act as huntsman or field master.

The Huntsman is a professional whose duty on the hunt is to find a fox and direct the pack. He should know and have the affection of each of his hounds and work them skillfully with voice and horn to keep them on the scent. He also supervises the *whippers-in* in their job of keeping hounds together.

The Field Master is charged with keeping the day's hunt running smoothly. Unlike the huntsman, who rides in the lead with full attention on the fox and the pack, the field master looks after the riders in the field, sees that gates are not left open, notes any damage to property, etc.

A DAY AFIELD

On the day of a hunt, the field assembles in the morning at the time and place designated. There is time for riders to greet, for a courteous salute to the Master of Fox Hounds. Close to the mounted huntsman hounds wait eagerly for the signal to move. They are numbered in two's; 12 "couple" means a pack of 24 hounds.

After the horn sounds and the field begins to move, there may be an uneventful ride of many minutes before a fox or a scent is found. Riders take these moments to appreciate the beauties of the day, the keenness and discipline of the pack, and the display of horsemanship by the other members of the field. It is not a time for "larking" (taking unnecessary jumps), though some restless young rider may give in to the temptation.

Suddenly the hounds give tongue; they have found a fresh scent and the field of riders holds back to let them work. Soon they start off on the line of the scent, the field following. The pace is restrained. There may be periods when the hounds lose the scent and the huntsman guides them in finding it again. With luck, they are soon running hot on the trail and in full cry. The chase is over streams, fences, stone walls, and meadows, and finally one of the riders in the field catches sight of the fox. Pack and field take after it at top speed, horses galloping, hounds baying. "Charley Fox" sets a lively pace, but the hounds are sure to outlast him unless he can elude them. If a kill comes, the riders at the front claim their trophies—mask, brush (tail), and paws of the fox. The huntsman may cast the pack again, or—if the day is late—sound the call for "going home."

Whipper-in rounds
up straying hound (left).
His duty on hunt
is to keep pack together.

13 | Rodeo

Rodeo these days is a sport that draws millions of paying customers, offers millions in prize money, and provides a year-round spectacle which has danger, color, and excitement. Back in the early 1800's, when Yankee cowboys first learned the tricks of herding longhorns from Mexican *vaqueros,* there were no rodeos, only informal contests spurred by the competitiveness of the cowpokes. Towns that sprang up along cattle-drive trails saw many a wild demonstration of roping, riding, and racing. As the cattle industry spread after the Civil War, these contests became more elaborate, involving teams from several ranches. Deer Trail, Colorado, hosted the first such competition in 1869. By the time of the Denver show of 1887—the first to which spectators had to pay admission—rodeo was firmly established as part of the Western scene.

The main events of the rodeo show the cowboy at work, roping runaway steers, throwing and tying calves, sticking on the back of an untamed horse. A smart horse is a great help to a rodeo contestant, and in bronc-riding contests a wild horse is a better test of ability. (The "bucking bronco" is a horse that has learned to hate the feel of a rider, usually because of harsh treatment in being broken to the saddle.)

There are some 600 shows on today's rodeo circuit. The "Big Four" outdoor shows are the Cheyenne "Frontier Days," the Pendleton, Oregon, Roundup, the Calgary Stampede, and the "California Rodeo" at Salinas. With opening parades, specialty acts, celebrity appearances, etc., they little resemble their rough-and-ready origins; but for riding and roping, the rodeo is, as much as ever, a thrilling view of the cowboy in action with the best cow ponies in all the West.

142

BAREBACK RIDING

In this event, the contestant slips onto his bronco inside a narrow chute, and gets a one-handed grip on the strap that circles the horse's barrel behind the front legs. Another strap circles the horse tightly just in front of the hind legs to provoke him into bucking more angrily. When the chute opens the rider spurs his bronco out into the arena. He is supposed to keep on spurring, and stay on for eight seconds. He cannot change hands on the grip strap and must keep his other hand well away from his body. If he is not thrown, a mounted pick-up man closes in and deftly swings him off his horse at the end of the ride.

Two judges, each with 50 points to award (25 for rider, 25 for horse), score the ride. Out of a possible 100 the average bronc-rider is happy to score in the 60's.

Preceding pages: Bulldogger about
to flip steer, with hazer
looking on. Above: Bronc gives
bareback rider rough time.

CALF ROPING

The next main event is calf roping, each contestant drawing lots for the calf he will rope. The trick is to catch the scampering calf cleanly with the first throw of the lariat, flip it on its side, and hitch three of its feet together—all in winning time. A top roper with a well-trained horse can do it in 12 or 13 seconds. He spurs his horse into action as soon as the calf crosses the starting line. Within a few feet of the animal he throws the rope he has had in readiness, one end tied to the saddle horn, the rest coiled in his right hand. As the calf is roped, the horse skids to a stop and the rider jumps to the ground. Twenty or 25 feet of line uncoil and the horse, backtracking if necessary, keeps it stretched taut between the calf and the saddle horn. The man spills his calf, whips the "pigging string"—a short rope—from his teeth, and makes the required tie of three of the calf's feet. Then he signals that he is through. If he has done the job in winning time, much credit must go to the horse.

SADDLE-BRONC RIDING

Central event of the rodeo is saddle-bronc riding, in which the horse carries a regulation Western saddle and the rider tries to stay in it for ten seconds, while spurring his horse on to buck wildly. He can hold on only with his legs. Like the bareback rider, he must keep one hand well away from his body; with the other he holds the reins. If he takes hold of the saddle or if either foot slips out of the stirrups, he will be disqualified. The reins are attached to a halter only; the horse wears no bit. The wilder the ride, the more points earned.

Roping events of rodeo
originated on open range.
Handy Quarter Horse
is asset to contestant at left.

BULLDOGGING

This event, also called steer wrestling, demonstrates the way to stop a steer if you don't happen to have a lasso handy. (See illustration, pages 140-141.) A young bull of 700 or 800 pounds is released. Two riders go after it—one, called a hazer, rides alongside the steer to keep it from veering away. On the other side rides the bulldogger, whose horse brings him skillfully abreast of the steer at just the right distance so that he will be in position for an easy fall on the animal. The bulldogger throws himself from his horse and brackets the steer's neck between his chest and outer arm. He crooks this arm around the steer's outside horn and grabs hold of the inside horn with his other hand. His feet are slipping from the stirrups well ahead of him to act as a break and to help him flip the steer as he thrusts down on the inside

146

Saddle-bronc riding
(above left) is favorite rodeo
event. Bull riding
(above right) is most dangerous.

horn. Done by a top performer, it can all be over in as little as five seconds.

A bulldogger needs a good horse, and if ridden on loan from another owner, the horse takes a share in the winnings.

BULL RIDING

In this, the climax of the rodeo, contestants try for an eight-second ride on the back of a bucking Brahma bull. A rope tied loosely around the bull's middle is the only hand-hold allowed. This is dangerous sport, since bulls are inclined to gore a rider who is thrown or dismounted. It is the job of the rodeo clowns to distract a bull during those tense moments. A bull ride, however, is almost always spectacular, and rodeo riders feel that the extra risk is worth it for the points they can pick up.

14 | Horse Shows

The horse show, as a comprehensive event for displaying the talents of horses and riders, was a late arrival among horse sports in America. A century ago horsemen showed their animals at local fairs. Today they have the spotlight all to themselves at more than 700 recognized shows, plus the countless informal events held countrywide throughout the season. The top competitors meet at week-long events such as the National Horse Show in New York, the Devon in Pennsylvania, the Washington (D.C.) International, the Kentucky State Fair at Louisville, the American Royal at Kansas City, and the Chicago International. Social events, silver trophies, and sizable cash prizes are features of these shows. On a smaller scale, but also important, are the hundreds of two-day shows, spaced out on the calendar so that exhibitors can travel the circuit, gaining points toward their season's totals.

Jumpers at Devon,
Pennsylvania, show. This is
annual event for
East's top horses and riders.

SHOW CIRCUIT

Horse shows are regulated by the American Horse Shows Association, founded in 1911. The AHSA sets down uniform rules for competition, passes on the eligibility of exhibitors, sets up the show calendar, oversees the fair treatment of riders and the humane treatment of horses, issues licenses to qualified judges and stewards, and records the results of competition. A "recognized" show—one sanctioned by the AHSA—has advantages both for management and riders. Procedures of class competition are clearly understood by all, and only exhibitors who meet AHSA standards of honesty may compete. Besides the licensed judges, stewards are on hand to see that the rules are observed. Also, the services of a veterinarian and a blacksmith are always provided.

To take account of regional differences in popularity of show divisions, the AHSA has organized the sport into 11 geographical zones. Within each zone committees are formed to represent the varying interests of horsemen. Committees include: Arabian, Combined Training Events, Dressage, Equitation, Hackney, Harness, Hunter, Jumper, Junior Exhibitors, Morgan, Palomino, Parade Horses, Polo, Roadster, Saddle Horse, Shetland Pony, Walking Horse, Welsh Pony, and Western.

A simple system of rating shows allows exhibitors to win points in proportion to the quality of their performance. The front-rank, week-long shows are rated "A"; as shows diminish in rank, offering fewer events and less prize money, they are rated "B" or "C" accordingly. Points won at an "A" show count twice as much as "B"-show points and four times as much as "C"-show points.

150

SHOW EVENTS

Horses are shown according both to their specialty and their breed. There are several classes within the larger divisions of events in a show. For example, the Hunter Division includes separate classes for performance, conformation, and correct appointments of horse and rider.

In the breed divisions, it is the horses themselves that are judged, not the skill of the rider. Horses are rated on their action in the customary gaits, and the degree to which they approach the ideal conformation of the breed. In the Palomino Division, Western tack may be required, while Arabians may have a class for riders in Eastern costume. Prospective exhibitors are guided by a show catalog listing all events, class specifications, and prizes offered.

Show competition
teaches young riders
a disciplined
approach to equitation.

EQUITATION

Equitation is a division in which young riders—up to 18 years of age, sometimes up to 21—display their horsemanship. The contestant should have a horse with the quality and spirit that will show his skill to advantage. Judges scrutinize the rider's form and his ability to bring forth a smooth and disciplined performance from his mount. Does the rider show "good hands," keeping a light but constant contact through the reins with his horse's mouth? Does he maintain poise and command throughout the required series of gaits and maneuvers? Can he perform as well on a strange mount? (Equitation competitors may be required to switch to a horse they do not know.) The seat—the rider's posture in the saddle—varies according to the way a horse is being used. In equitation classes three types of seats are demonstrated: the hunter seat, the saddle-horse seat, and the Western stock seat. Routines for saddle and stock seats require—besides performance at the normal gaits—drills such as figure eights, circles, and serpentines. Hunter-seat contestants must show their skill over jumps.

For keen competition, equitation contestants at organized shows are usually matched according to age or level of accomplishment. A maiden class is for riders who have yet to win a blue ribbon (first prize) in a particular division. Novice class is open to riders seeking their third blue ribbon, and limit class to riders seeking their sixth. An open class is one in which all riders under the age limit may compete at equitation. The dream of all young equitation riders is to win one of the national championship prizes, such as the Maclay Cup for hunter-seat performance.

DRESSAGE

America was slow to take up the art of dressage (a word that means *training* in French). The French and Germans developed this highly refined technique of equine calisthenics for horse and rider, and the supreme demonstration of dressage remains that of the famous Spanish Riding School of Vienna, with its magnificent Lippizan horses. The object of the exercises of dressage is to give a horse balance, great muscular flexibility, and perfect response to the most subtle commands of an accomplished rider. Entrants put their mounts through a series of drills over a flat course. Commands to the horse must not be perceptible to viewers.

Dressage Movements

Pirouette: Feet moving usually in a canter, horse moves forequarters in a circle while hind feet continue in motion at center of the circle, hitting same place on the ground.

Passage: A highly elevated trot, evenly cadenced, with brief hesitation of the feet at upper point of lift.

Piaffe: A trot in place, without moving forward.

Shoulder in: Horse trots along wall of ring with head and shoulders curved toward center of ring and haunches parallel to wall. Inside legs cross over in front of outside legs.

Haunches in (travers): Horse moves with head and shoulders parallel to wall and haunches curved toward center of ring. Outside legs cross over inside legs.

Haunches out (renvers): Horse moves with head and shoulders parallel to wall and haunches curved toward wall.

Pass or **transversal:** Horse trots at an oblique forward line, head bent slightly in direction of movement.

HUNTER DIVISION

Hunter Division events test horses over a course designed to simulate the hunting field, with jumps representing stone walls, picket fences, hedges, gates, etc. Here, it is the animal's performance, not the rider's horsemanship, that counts. A great variety of classes provides fair competition for horses of every description, according to age, experience, and weight. Professional trainers with horses for sale are keen exhibitors in the classes for green and young hunters. Qualified Hunter class is for horses that have been hunted regularly with a recognized pack, while Working Hunter Class is open to all, whether qualified or not; they are usually divided into lightweights, middleweights, or heavyweights, depending on their ability to carry up to 165, 185, or more pounds respectively. In the Model Hunter Class a horse is shown without saddle or rider and is judged solely on conformation. Appointments classes require the display of every traditional item of livery, tack, and field equipment: whip and spurs, flask and sandwich case, gloves and hat, etc. The Corinthian Class is an appointments event in which every rider is required to be a member of an active, recognized hunt.

Jumps in the Hunter Division range from 3 feet, required of young or inexperienced horses, to 4 feet 6 inches for seasoned animals. The hunter is judged on the "brilliancy" —the ease and smoothness—of his jumping style. He should approach the barriers in stride and fly over them gracefully with just enough room to spare. Hesitation and awkwardness will be penalized. Hunters may also be judged on manners, way of going, quality, substance, and soundness.

154

Lady sidesaddle rider shows her hunter in appointments class, with required top hat, sandwich case, gloves, etc.

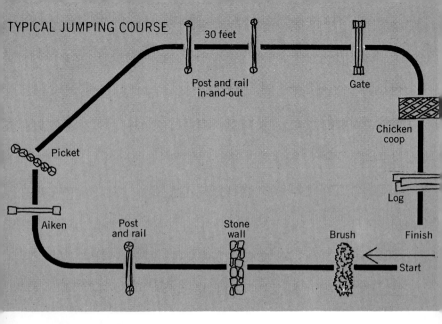

TYPICAL JUMPING COURSE

30 feet

Post and rail
in-and-out

Gate

Chicken
coop

Picket

Log

Aiken

Post
and rail

Stone
wall

Brush

Finish

Start

WESTERN DIVISION

Popular Western Division events sometimes fill half the bill of an Eastern show. The horse trained for working cows should be agile and responsive, with a quiet, take-charge manner about his task. In cutting events, the horse must separate a cow from the group. He is rated on how he works the cow and responds to the reins, also on conformation, manners, and appointments.

In roping events the rider has two minutes to work and may throw repeated loops. The horse should close quickly on the calf and, as soon as it is roped and the rider slips to the ground, back up and stand so that the rope attached to the saddle horn is kept taut.

Reining performance is a specialty of some stock horses. A typical reining pattern calls for the horse to gallop, halt, back up, ride through several figures, pivot to right and

156

left, and roll back on his hocks to right and left.

Barrel racing is a timed event for lady riders in which contestants must race around each of three barrels set out on the course in a triangular pattern.

In stock-seat equitation, appointments and riders' performance are deciding factors. Parade Horses are judged principally on style in the walk and parade gait—a stately, elevated trot; quality, manners, and appointments count too.

In Western pleasure and trail riding classes, horses must walk, jog, lope, and navigate obstacles.

Finally there are the model and halter classes, in which breed winners are chosen on the basis of conformation, quality, substance, and soundness.

JUMPER DIVISION

Jumping contests are scored on performance only. A horse of any description can win if he takes more jumps more soundly than the competition. His rider's style—or lack of it —does not count, although the rider's skill is crucial to winning. Events are decided as surviving horses jump repeated rounds over higher and higher barriers.

Some shows have classes for maiden, novice, and limit jumpers, but ordinarily horses are grouped as either green or open jumpers. Green jumpers are those that have not been shown in the Jumper Division at a recognized show earlier than January 1st of the current year. They are tested over jumps of about 3 feet 9 inches. Open jumpers are those shown—usually by professional riders—in the open-to-all class. These are seasoned horses for whom six-foot jumps are everyday work.

A typical course tests the horse's pacing with barriers placed at irregular intervals; it tests his calm with obstacles that are visually alarming, such as brightly painted barrels; it tests his power and co-ordination with vertical or broad jumps of increasing difficulty.

The winner in a jumping class is the horse that has committed the fewest faults. Under AHSA rules there is a specified penalty for every fault, such as touching an obstacle, knocking it down, refusing a jump, etc.

Some shows judge jumping competition according to the international rules set down by the *Fédération Equestre Internationale* (the FEI, of which the AHSA is a member). The two sets of rules diverge on many points. Under AHSA rules, the time of a round is not usually a factor in winning, nor is there any minimum weight to be carried by competing jumpers. Elimination follows a fall by either horse or rider or both. In shows governed by international rules, such as the Olympics and the Pan American games, rounds are clocked, and jumpers must carry a specified minimum weight; a fall costs the contestant eight faults, but not elimination, and touches of the obstacles do not count.

Two traditional jumping events in American shows are the Touch-and-Out, in which the contestant is required to leave the ring as soon as he touches an obstacle, and the Knock-Down-and-Out, in which he is put out for knocking down an obstacle. In each event the rider with the highest tally of clean jumps wins. The High Jump is a thrilling single-jump event in which the barrier is gradually raised. Horses that fail to clear it in three tries are eliminated. The winner is the horse that clears the highest mark.

INDEX: *Caption references in italics*

159

160